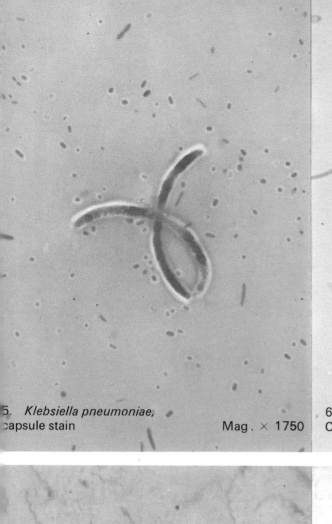

5. *Klebsiella pneumoniae,*
capsule stain
Mag. × 1750

6. *Clostridium sporogenes,*
Conklins spore stain
Mag. × 1800

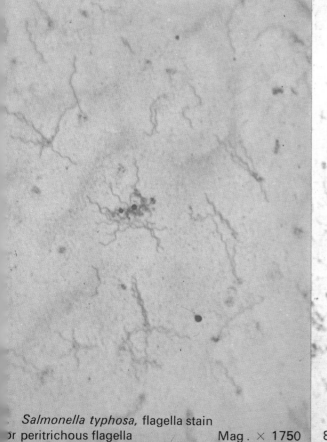

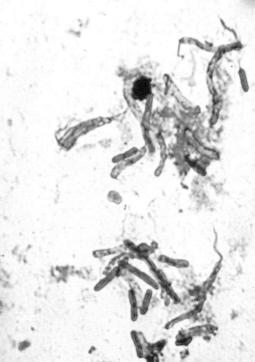

Salmonella typhosa, flagella stain
or peritrichous flagella
Mag. × 1750

8. *Rhodospirillum rubrum,* for flagella
Mag. × 1700

AN ATLAS OF PLANT STRUCTURE: VOLUME 2

by W. H. Freeman and Brian Bracegirdle
An Atlas of Invertebrate Structure
An Atlas of Embryology
An Atlas of Histology
An Advanced Atlas of Histology

by Brian Bracegirdle and Patricia H. Miles
An Atlas of Plant Structure: Volume 1
An Atlas of Plant Structure: Volume 2
An Atlas of Chordate Structure

AN ATLAS OF

Plant Structure

Volume 2

Brian Bracegirdle *BSc PhD FIBiol FRPS*

and

Patricia H Miles *MSc MIBiol ARPS*

Heinemann Educational Books
London

Heinemann Educational Books Ltd
22 Bedford Square, London WC1B 3HH

London Edinburgh Melbourne Auckland
Hong Kong Singapore Kuala Lumpur New Delhi
Ibadan Nairobi Johannesburg
Exeter (NH) Kingston Port of Spain

ISBN 0 435 60314 0

First published 1973
Reprinted 1976, 1978, 1981

Printed and bound in Hong Kong by
Wing King Tong Co. Ltd

Preface

This second volume completes the work on plant structure and is designed, like the first, to be used at the laboratory bench to help the student interpret his own material. It is not intended to supplant the usual textbooks, but to guide the student before he turns to them for further theoretical information.

In addition to providing a wide coverage of species and structures, we have included material useful to the student concerned with the gross plant—for example, flower and fruit anatomy to complement work with a flora. Examples of the notable difference in appearance between living and prepared specimens have been shown, and special illumination used to make clear the structure of certain specimens.

The same techniques of photography and independent drawing have been used as in the first volume, and we have again been fortunate in having our own collections of preparations augmented by Philip Harris Biological Supplies Ltd and the Polytechnic of Central London; we are sincerely indebted to our friends in those places. John Haller has given freely of his time and experience, and has provided material from his own collection to fill gaps otherwise unfilled; we owe him much gratitude.

John Juniper and Clive Wyborn have again saved us from error and given their enthusiastic support from the very beginning. We are most sincerely grateful to them both:

1973

B. B.
P. H. M.

COLOUR TRANSPARENCIES FOR PROJECTION

Every picture in this book is available as a 2 × 2 colour slide for projection from *Philip Harris Biological Supplies Ltd, Oldmixon, Weston-super-Mare, Avon*

The original master transparencies were made at the same time as the negatives for the pictures in this book, exclusively for this company. The authors recommend these slides for their quality and moderate cost as excellent aids to the teaching of plant structure especially in conjunction with this book.

Contents

ROOTS

LEAVES

REPRODUCTIVE STRUCTURES

AN ATLAS OF
Plant Structure

Volume 2

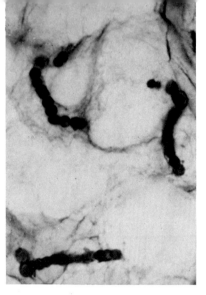

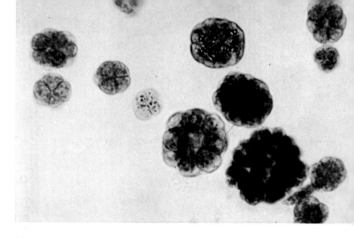

9. **Nostoc**, LS. Mag. ×400

10. **Pandorina**, E, prepared slide. Mag. ×450

11. **Pandorina**, E, living, phase contrast/flash. Mag. ×550

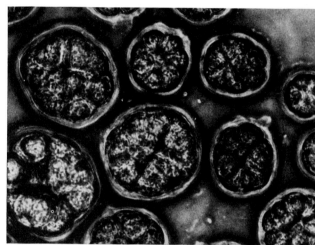

12. **Eudorina**, E, prepared slide. Mag. ×450

13. **Eudorina**, E, living, phase contrast/flash. Mag. ×550

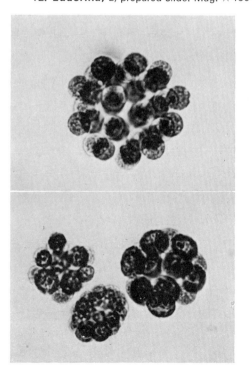

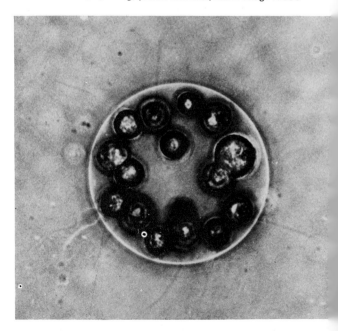

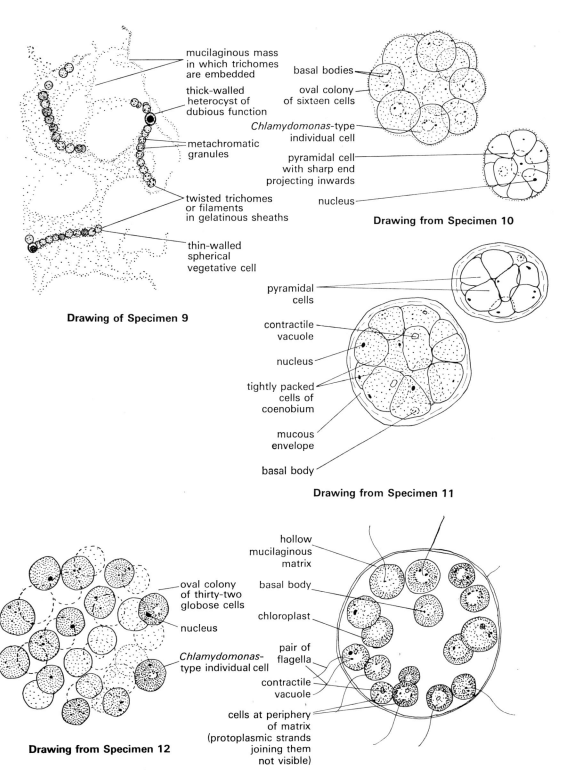

mucilaginous mass
in which trichomes
are embedded

thick-walled
heterocyst of
dubious function

metachromatic
granules

twisted trichomes
or filaments
in gelatinous sheaths

thin-walled
spherical
vegetative cell

Drawing of Specimen 9

basal bodies

oval colony
of sixteen cells

Chlamydomonas-type
individual cell

pyramidal cell
with sharp end
projecting inwards

nucleus

Drawing from Specimen 10

pyramidal
cells

contractile
vacuole

nucleus

tightly packed
cells of
coenobium

mucous
envelope

basal body

Drawing from Specimen 11

oval colony
of thirty-two
globose cells

nucleus

Chlamydomonas-
type individual cell

Drawing from Specimen 12

hollow
mucilaginous
matrix

basal body

chloroplast

pair of
flagella

contractile
vacuole

cells at periphery
of matrix
(protoplasmic strands
joining them
not visible)

Drawing of Specimen 13

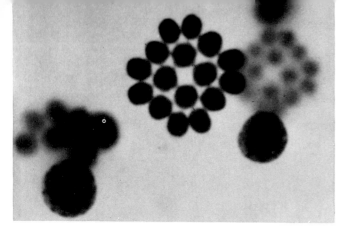

14. *Gonium*, E, prepared slide. Mag. ×400

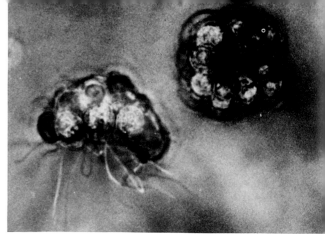

15. *Gonium*, E, living, phase contrast/flash. Mag. ×400

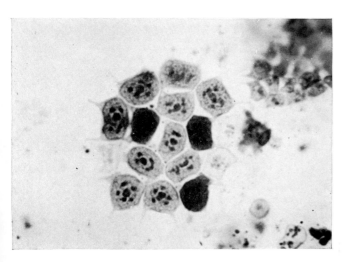

16. *Pediastrum*, prepared slide. Mag. ×400

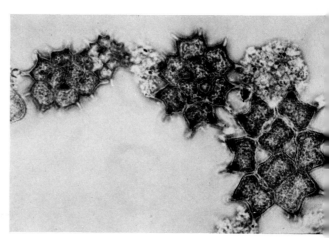

17. *Pediastrum*, E, living, phase contrast/flash. Mag. ×400

19. *Hydrodictyon*, living, phase contrast/flash. Mag. ×220

18. *Hydrodictyon*, prepared slide. Mag. 5×12

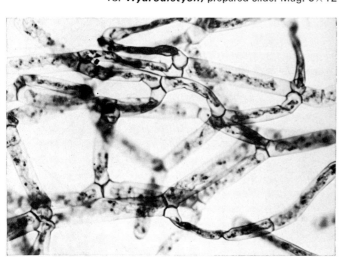

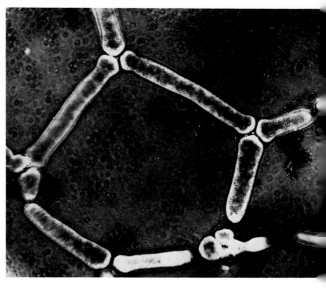

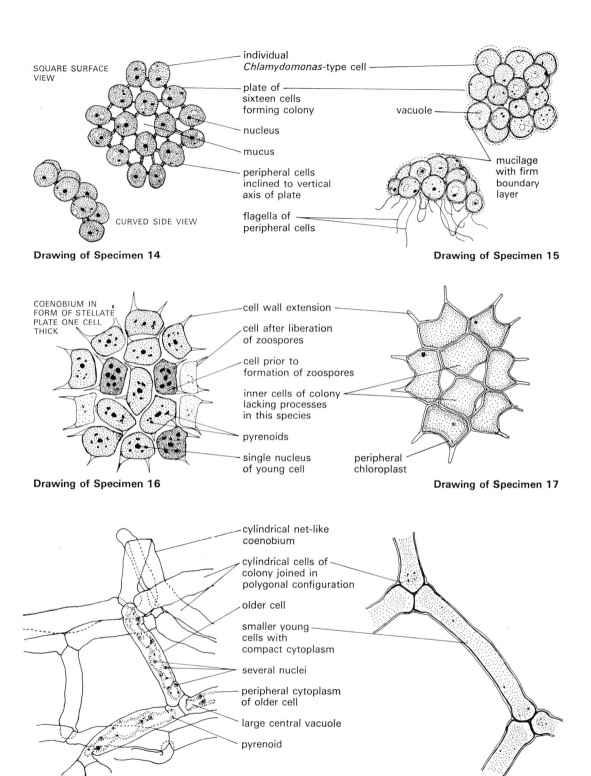

SQUARE SURFACE VIEW

individual *Chlamydomonas*-type cell

plate of sixteen cells forming colony

nucleus

mucus

peripheral cells inclined to vertical axis of plate

CURVED SIDE VIEW

flagella of peripheral cells

Drawing of Specimen 14

vacuole

mucilage with firm boundary layer

Drawing of Specimen 15

COENOBIUM IN FORM OF STELLATE PLATE ONE CELL THICK

cell wall extension

cell after liberation of zoospores

cell prior to formation of zoospores

inner cells of colony lacking processes in this species

pyrenoids

single nucleus of young cell

peripheral chloroplast

Drawing of Specimen 16

Drawing of Specimen 17

cylindrical net-like coenobium

cylindrical cells of colony joined in polygonal configuration

older cell

smaller young cells with compact cytoplasm

several nuclei

peripheral cytoplasm of older cell

large central vacuole

pyrenoid

Drawing of Specimen 18

Drawing of Specimen 19

20. ***Scenedesmus***, prepared slide. Mag. ×995

21. ***Cladophora***, vegetative structure, prepared slide. Mag. ×350

22. ***Cladophora***, asexual stages, prepared slide, oblique illumination. Mag. ×550

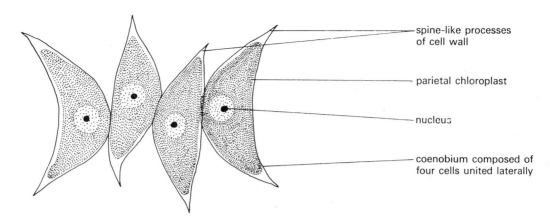

spine-like processes
of cell wall

parietal chloroplast

nucleus

coenobium composed of
four cells united laterally

Drawing of Specimen 20

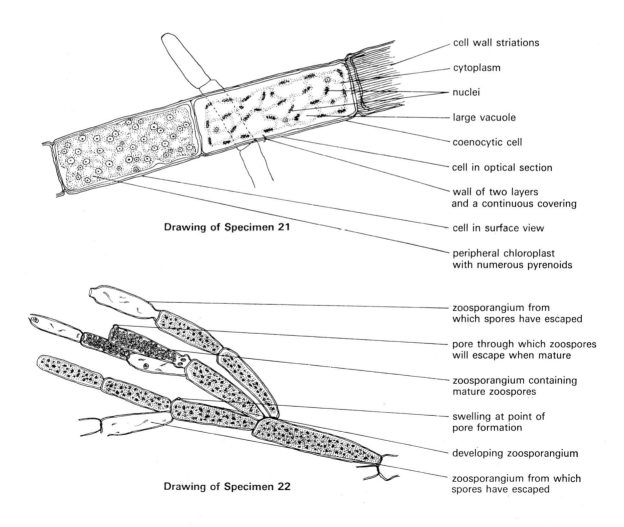

cell wall striations

cytoplasm

nuclei

large vacuole

coenocytic cell

cell in optical section

wall of two layers
and a continuous covering

cell in surface view

peripheral chloroplast
with numerous pyrenoids

Drawing of Specimen 21

zoosporangium from
which spores have escaped

pore through which zoospores
will escape when mature

zoosporangium containing
mature zoospores

swelling at point of
pore formation

developing zoosporangium

zoosporangium from which
spores have escaped

Drawing of Specimen 22

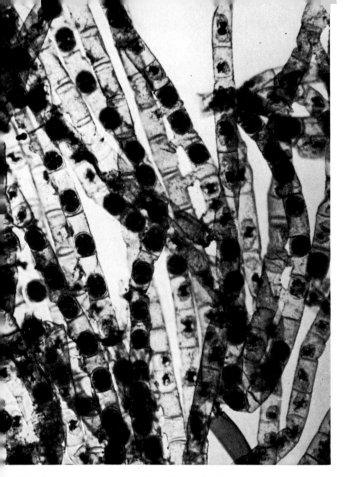

24. **Zygnema**, prepared slide. Mag. ×200

25. **Zygnema**, living, phase contrast/flash. Mag. ×325

23. **Pleurococcus**, E, prepared slide. Mag. ×750

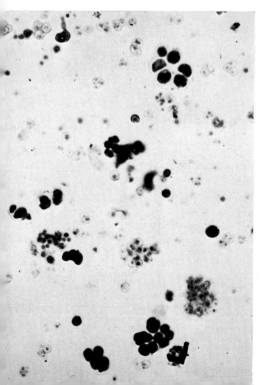

26. **Closterium**, prepared slide. Mag. ×450

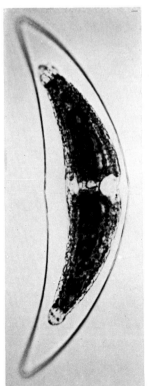

27. **Closterium**, living, phase contrast/flash. Mag. ×600

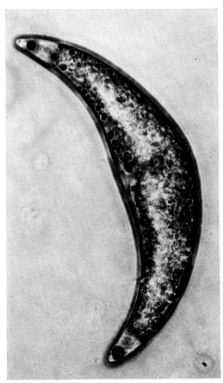

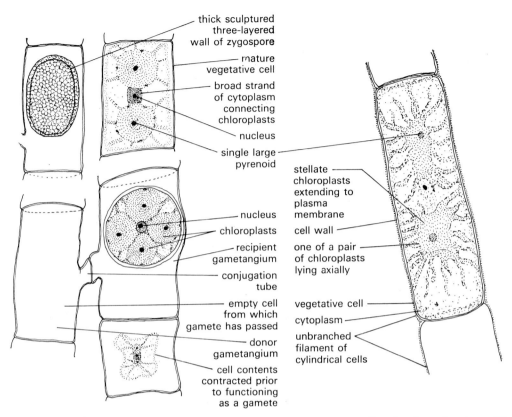

thick sculptured
three-layered
wall of zygospore

mature
vegetative cell

broad strand
of cytoplasm
connecting
chloroplasts

nucleus

single large
pyrenoid

stellate
chloroplasts
extending to
plasma
membrane

cell wall

nucleus

chloroplasts

recipient
gametangium

conjugation
tube

one of a pair
of chloroplasts
lying axially

vegetative cell

cytoplasm

empty cell
from which
gamete has passed

unbranched
filament of
cylindrical cells

donor
gametangium

cell contents
contracted prior
to functioning
as a gamete

Details from Specimen 24

Drawing from Specimen 25

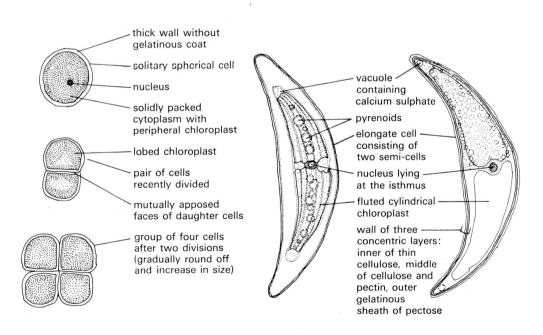

thick wall without
gelatinous coat

solitary spherical cell

nucleus

solidly packed
cytoplasm with
peripheral chloroplast

lobed chloroplast

pair of cells
recently divided

mutually apposed
faces of daughter cells

group of four cells
after two divisions
(gradually round off
and increase in size)

vacuole
containing
calcium sulphate

pyrenoids

elongate cell
consisting of
two semi-cells

nucleus lying
at the isthmus

fluted cylindrical
chloroplast

wall of three
concentric layers:
inner of thin
cellulose, middle
of cellulose and
pectin, outer
gelatinous
sheath of pectose

Details from Specimen 23

Drawing of Specimen 26

Drawing of Specimen 27

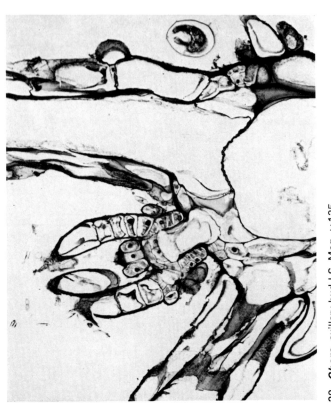

28. *Chara,* axillary bud LS. Mag. ×125

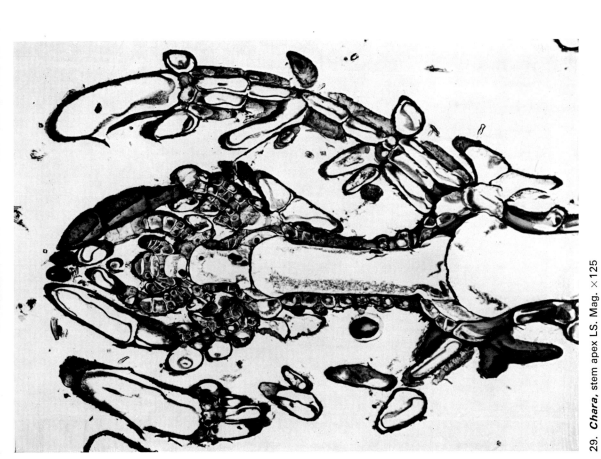

30. *Chara,* axil LS. Mag. ×125

29. *Chara,* stem apex LS. Mag. ×125

internode of
main axis

axillary
reproductive
branch

young
reproductive
organs

branch

Drawing of Specimen 28

corona

spirally elongate
enveloping
cells

oosphere

oogonium containing
one egg

branch
internode

pedicel

node

antheridial filament

shield cell

capitulum

Drawing of Specimen 30

apical cell
of branch

apical cell
of stem

nodal cells
peripheral cell
internodal cell

branch node

branch internode

cortical cells

branch axil

main axis

Drawing of Specimen 29

11

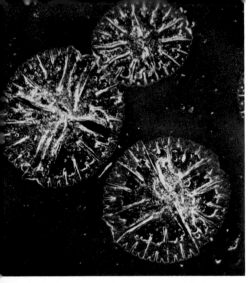

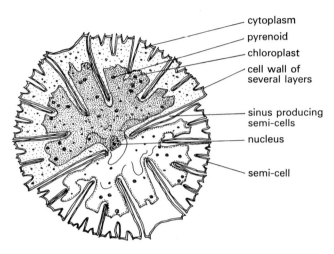

cytoplasm
pyrenoid
chloroplast
cell wall of
several layers

sinus producing
semi-cells

nucleus

semi-cell

1. *Micrasterias*, E, Rheinberg illumination. Mag. × 225

Drawing of Specimen 31

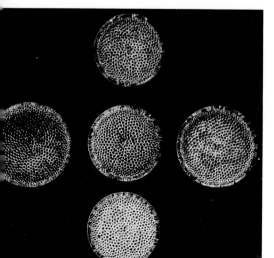

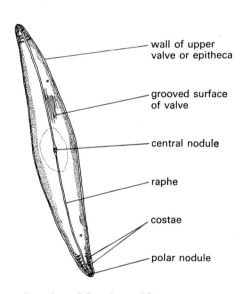

wall of upper
valve or epitheca

grooved surface
of valve

central nodule

raphe

costae

polar nodule

Drawing of Specimen 32

32. *Pleurosigma angulatum,* cleaned,
Rheinberg illumination. Mag. × 425

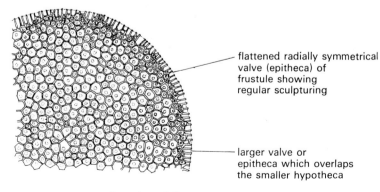

flattened radially symmetrical
valve (epitheca) of
frustule showing
regular sculpturing

larger valve or
epitheca which overlaps
the smaller hypotheca

Drawing of Specimen 33

33. *Coscinodiscus,* cleaned, Rheinberg illumination. Mag. × 350

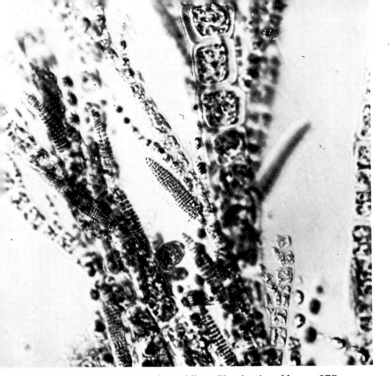

34. *Ectocarpus*, reproductive, oblique illumination. Mag. ×375

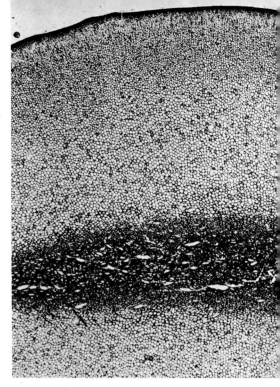

35. *Laminaria*, stipe TS. Mag. ×75

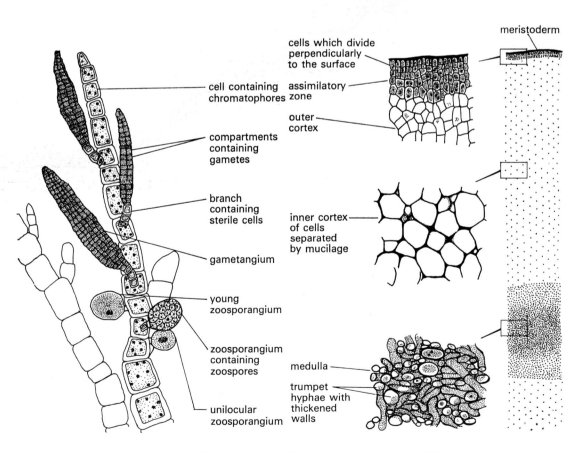

cells which divide perpendicularly to the surface

cell containing chromatophores

assimilatory zone

meristoderm

outer cortex

compartments containing gametes

branch containing sterile cells

inner cortex of cells separated by mucilage

gametangium

young zoosporangium

zoosporangium containing zoospores

medulla

trumpet hyphae with thickened walls

unilocular zoosporangium

Drawing from Specimen 34

Drawings from Specimen 35

13

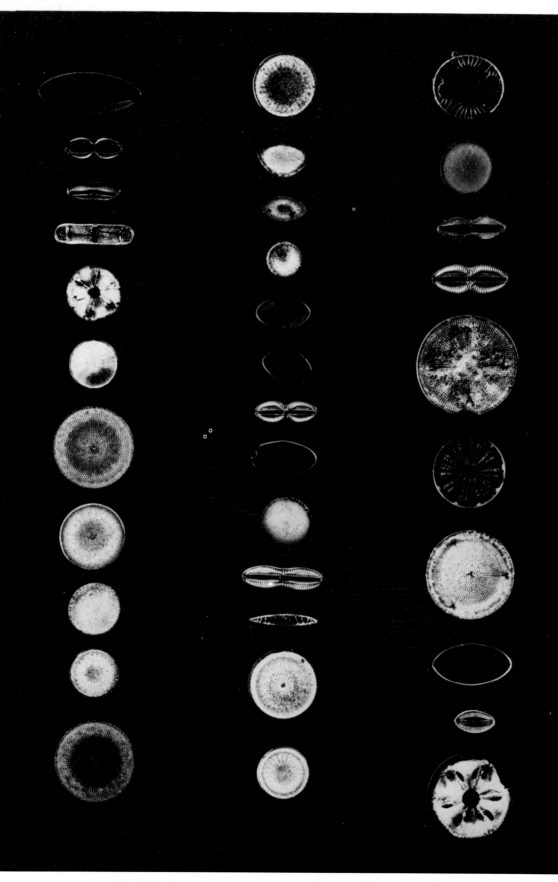

36. **Diatoms,** type specimens, cleaned, Rheinberg illumination. Mag. ×70

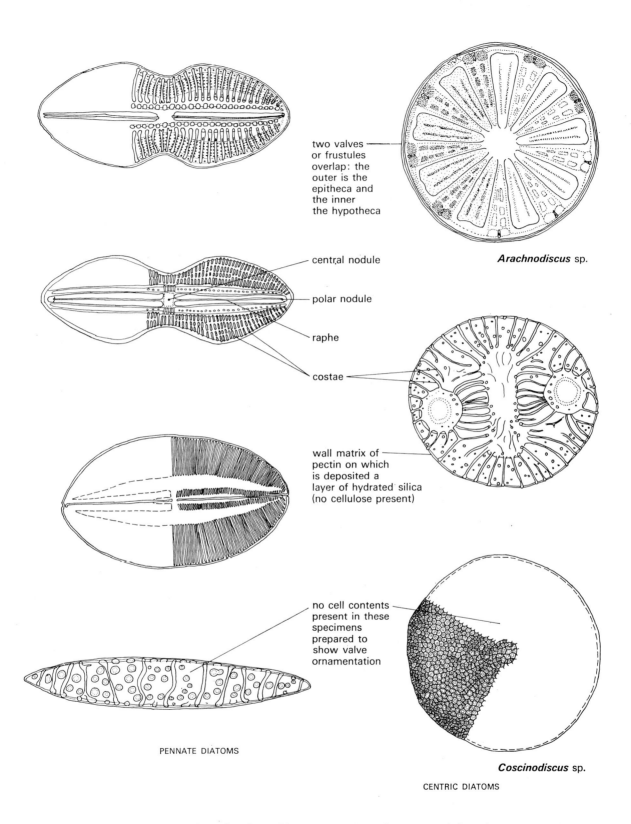

two valves
or frustules
overlap: the
outer is the
epitheca and
the inner
the hypotheca

Arachnodiscus sp.

central nodule

polar nodule

raphe

costae

wall matrix of
pectin on which
is deposited a
layer of hydrated silica
(no cellulose present)

no cell contents
present in these
specimens
prepared to
show valve
ornamentation

PENNATE DIATOMS

Coscinodiscus sp.

CENTRIC DIATOMS

Drawings from Specimen 36 to show variety of structure of frustules

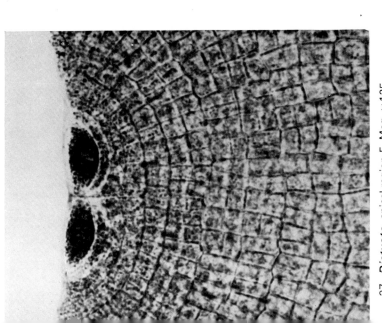

38. *Dictyota*, antheridia LS. Mag. ×250

39. *Dictyota*, oogonia LS. Mag. ×250

37. *Dictyota*, apical region E. Mag. ×125

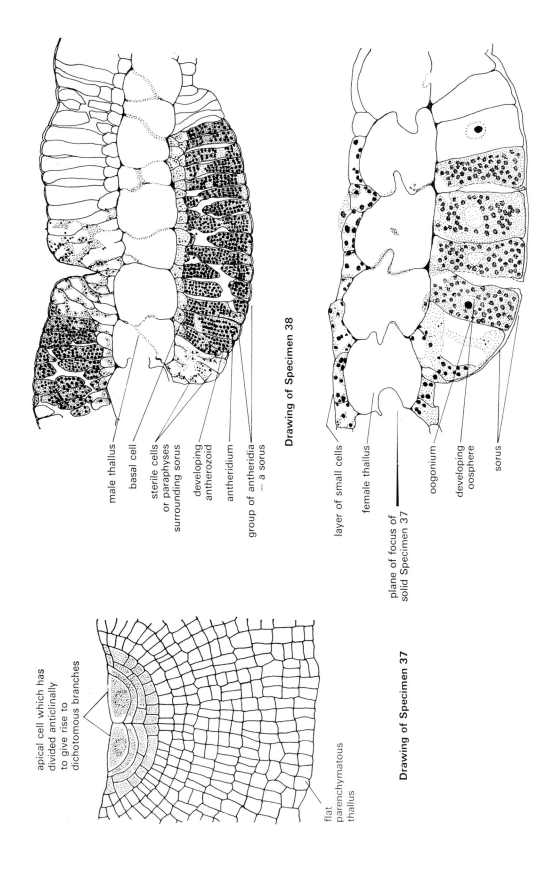

male thallus

basal cell

sterile cells
or paraphyses
surrounding sorus

developing
antherozoid

antheridium

group of antheridia
— a sorus

Drawing of Specimen 38

layer of small cells

female thallus

plane of focus of
solid Specimen 37

oogonium

developing
oosphere

sorus

Drawing of Specimen 39

apical cell which has
divided anticlinally
to give rise to
dichotomous branches

flat
parenchymatous
thallus

Drawing of Specimen 37

17

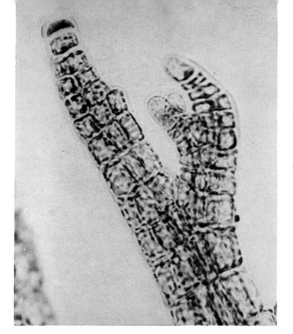

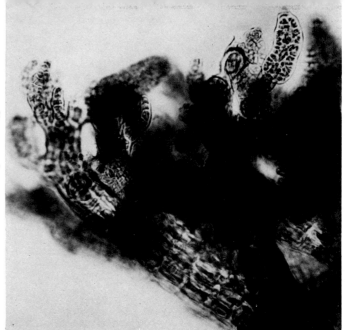

40. **Polysiphonia,** apical region E. Mag. ×375

41. **Polysiphonia,** antheridia E. Mag. ×375

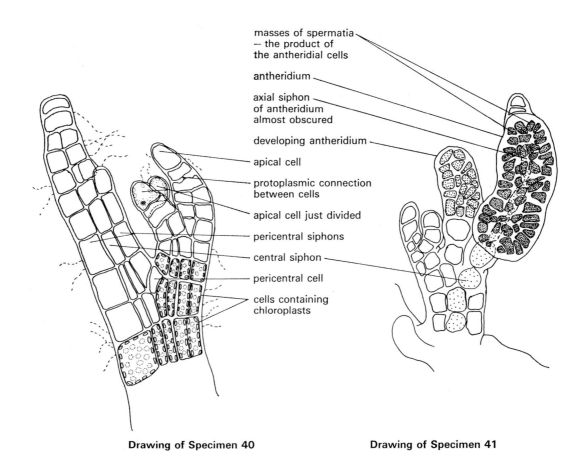

masses of spermatia
— the product of
the antheridial cells

antheridium

axial siphon
of antheridium
almost obscured

developing antheridium

apical cell

protoplasmic connection
between cells

apical cell just divided

pericentral siphons

central siphon

pericentral cell

cells containing
chloroplasts

Drawing of Specimen 40

Drawing of Specimen 41

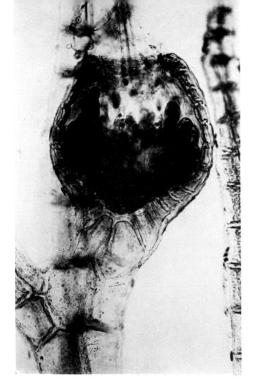

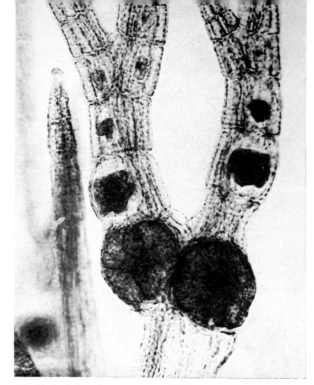

42. **Polysiphonia,** carpocyst E. Mag. ×375

43. **Polysiphonia,** tetraspores E. Mag. ×375

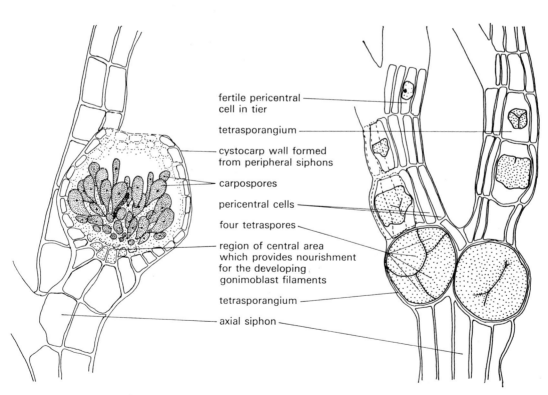

fertile pericentral cell in tier

tetrasporangium

cystocarp wall formed from peripheral siphons

carpospores

pericentral cells

four tetraspores

region of central area which provides nourishment for the developing gonimoblast filaments

tetrasporangium

axial siphon

Drawing of Specimen 42

Drawing of Specimen 43

44. **Algae,** gross specimens. Mag. ×2

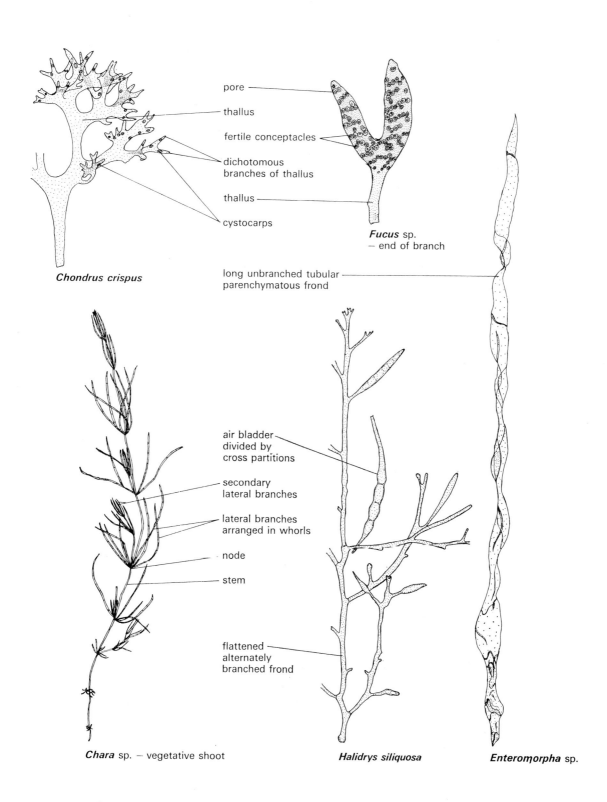

pore

thallus

fertile conceptacles

dichotomous
branches of thallus

thallus

cystocarps

Fucus sp.
– end of branch

Chondrus crispus

long unbranched tubular
parenchymatous frond

air bladder
divided by
cross partitions

secondary
lateral branches

lateral branches
arranged in whorls

node

stem

flattened
alternately
branched frond

Chara sp. – vegetative shoot

Halidrys siliquosa

Enteromorpha sp.

Drawing of Specimen 44

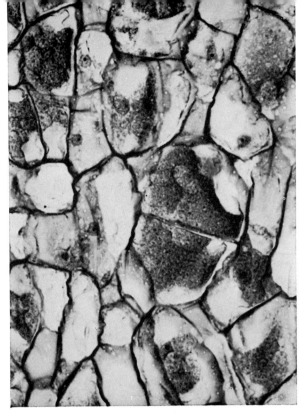

45. *Plasmodiophora*, plasmodium in TS host cells.
Mag. ×175

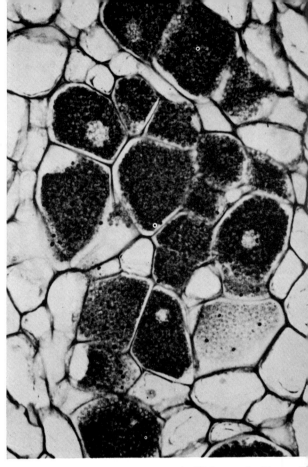

46. *Plasmodiophora*, spore stage in TS host cells. Mag. ×1⁷

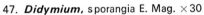

47. *Didymium*, sporangia E. Mag. ×30

48. *Synchitrium*, in TS host cells. Mag. ×150

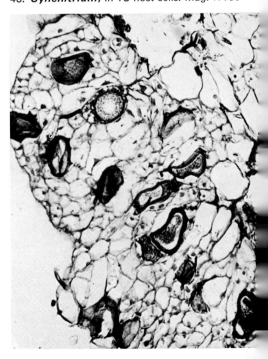

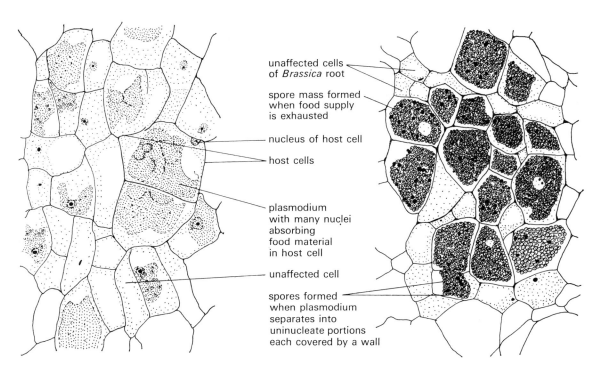

unaffected cells of *Brassica* root

spore mass formed when food supply is exhausted

nucleus of host cell

host cells

plasmodium with many nuclei absorbing food material in host cell

unaffected cell

spores formed when plasmodium separates into uninucleate portions each covered by a wall

Drawing of Specimen 45

Drawing of Specimen 46

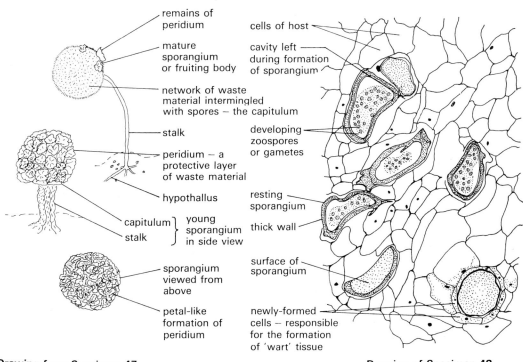

remains of peridium

mature sporangium or fruiting body

network of waste material intermingled with spores – the capitulum

stalk

peridium – a protective layer of waste material

hypothallus

capitulum } young
stalk } sporangium in side view

sporangium viewed from above

petal-like formation of peridium

cells of host

cavity left during formation of sporangium

developing zoospores or gametes

resting sporangium

thick wall

surface of sporangium

newly-formed cells – responsible for the formation of 'wart' tissue

Drawing from Specimen 47

Drawing of Specimen 48

52. **Pythium**, zoosporangia E. Mag. ×200

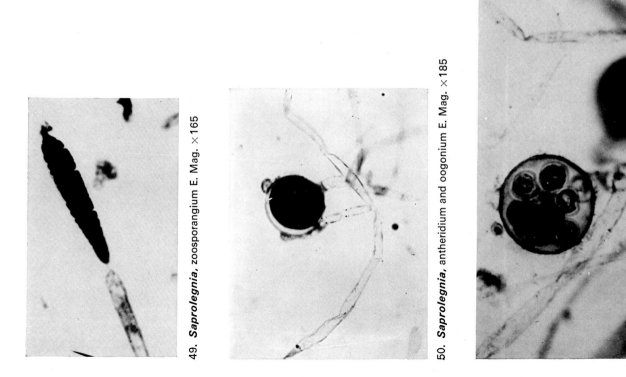

49. **Saprolegnia**, zoosporangium E. Mag. ×165

50. **Saprolegnia**, antheridium and oogonium E. Mag. ×185

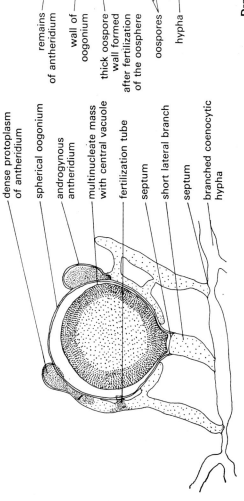

Drawings from Specimen 49

- zoospores escaping through opening at tip
- uninucleate zoospores
- sporangium
- zoosporangium proliferating at tip of hypha
- dense protoplasm
- septum
- hypha

A

B

Drawings from Specimen 52

- vesicle
- developing zoospores
- zoosporangium
- septum
- hypha
- zoosporangium
- vesicle
- contents passing into vesicle
- empty zoosporangium

A

B

C

Drawing of Specimen 50

- dense protoplasm of antheridium
- spherical oogonium
- androgynous antheridium
- multinucleate mass with central vacuole
- fertilization tube
- septum
- short lateral branch
- septum
- branched coenocytic hypha

Drawing of Specimen 51

- remains of antheridium
- wall of oogonium
- thick oospore wall formed after fertilization of the oosphere
- oospores
- hypha

25

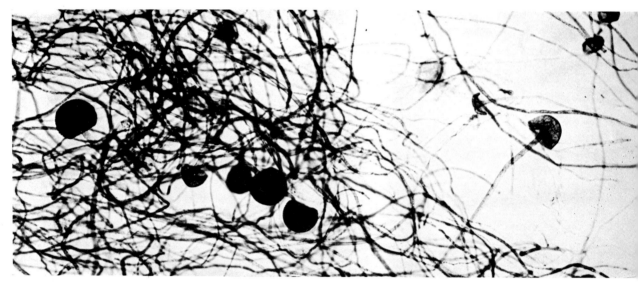

53. *Rhizopus,* asexual stages E. Mag. ×150

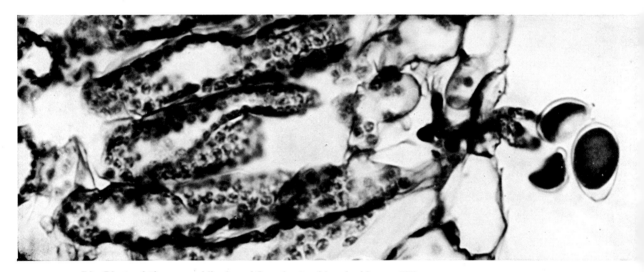

54. *Phytophthora,* conidiophore LS on host epidermis. Mag. ×550

55. *Sordaria,* perithecium VS. Mag. ×200

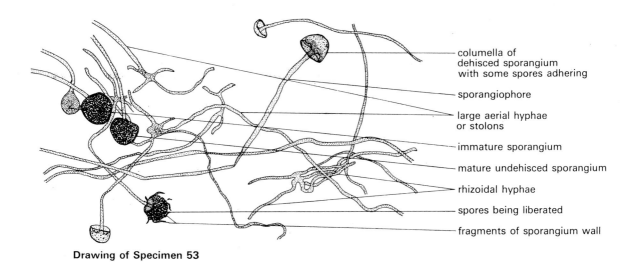

columella of
dehisced sporangium
with some spores adhering

sporangiophore

large aerial hyphae
or stolons

immature sporangium

mature undehisced sporangium

rhizoidal hyphae

spores being liberated

fragments of sporangium wall

Drawing of Specimen 53

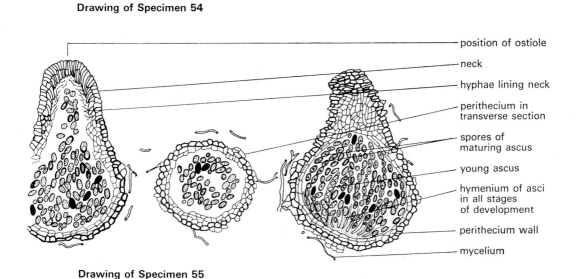

sub-stomatal cavity

branched conidiophore

guard cells of stoma

false conidium (zoosporangium)

intercellular mycelium

host epidermis

Drawing of Specimen 54

position of ostiole

neck

hyphae lining neck

perithecium in
transverse section

spores of
maturing ascus

young ascus

hymenium of asci
in all stages
of development

perithecium wall

mycelium

Drawing of Specimen 55

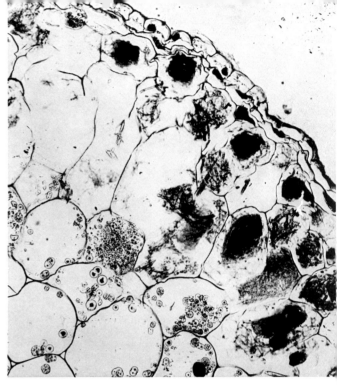

56. **Mycorrhiza,** ectotrophic on host roots. Mag. ×75

57. **Mycorrhiza,** endotrophic in host cells. Mag. ×250

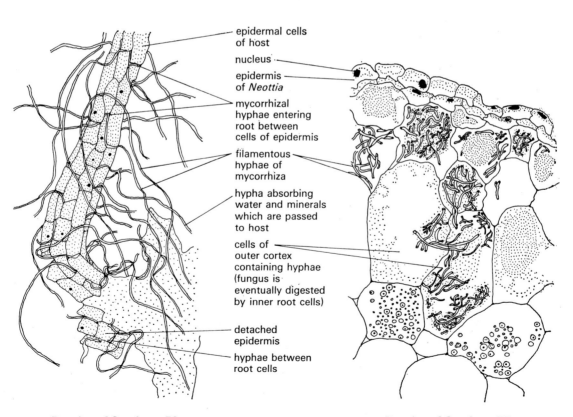

epidermal cells
of host

nucleus

epidermis
of *Neottia*

mycorrhizal
hyphae entering
root between
cells of epidermis

filamentous
hyphae of
mycorrhiza

hypha absorbing
water and minerals
which are passed
to host

cells of
outer cortex
containing hyphae
(fungus is
eventually digested
by inner root cells)

detached
epidermis

hyphae between
root cells

Drawing of Specimen 56

Drawing of Specimen 57

58. *Monilia,* conidiophores VS on host. Mag. ×350

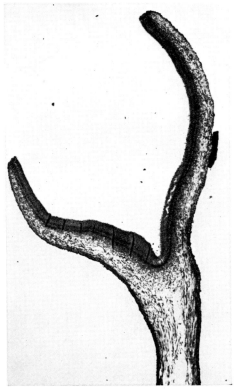

59. *Sclerotinia,* apothecium LS. Mag. ×30

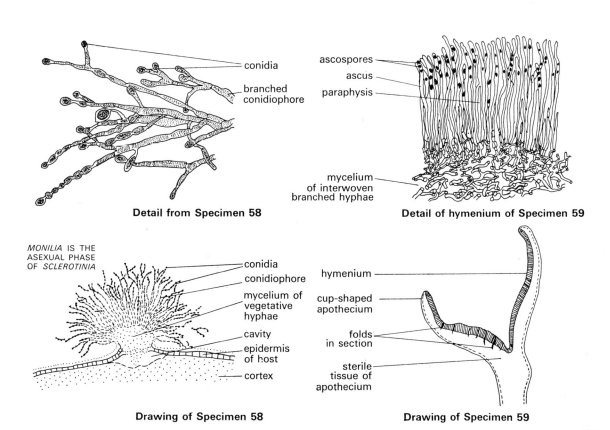

conidia

branched
conidiophore

Detail from Specimen 58

ascospores

ascus

paraphysis

mycelium
of interwoven
branched hyphae

Detail of hymenium of Specimen 59

MONILIA IS THE
ASEXUAL PHASE
OF *SCLEROTINIA*

conidia
conidiophore
mycelium of
vegetative
hyphae
cavity
epidermis
of host
cortex

Drawing of Specimen 58

hymenium

cup-shaped
apothecium

folds
in section

sterile
tissue of
apothecium

Drawing of Specimen 59

60. **Fungi,** gross specimens. Mag. ×2

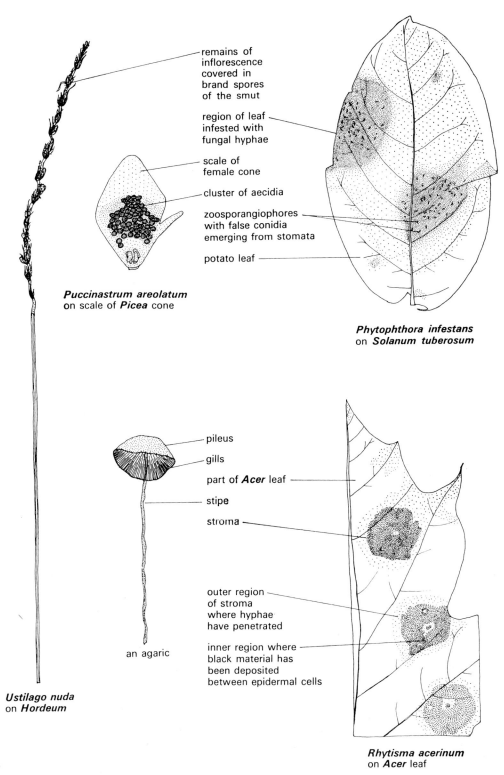

remains of
inflorescence
covered in
brand spores
of the smut

region of leaf
infested with
fungal hyphae

scale of
female cone

cluster of aecidia

zoosporangiophores
with false conidia
emerging from stomata

potato leaf

Puccinastrum areolatum
on scale of **Picea** cone

Phytophthora infestans
on **Solanum tuberosum**

pileus

gills

part of **Acer** leaf

stipe

stroma

outer region
of stroma
where hyphae
have penetrated

inner region where
black material has
been deposited
between epidermal cells

an agaric

Ustilago nuda
on **Hordeum**

Rhytisma acerinum
on **Acer** leaf

Drawing of Specimen 60

61. Lichens, gross specimens. Mag. ×2

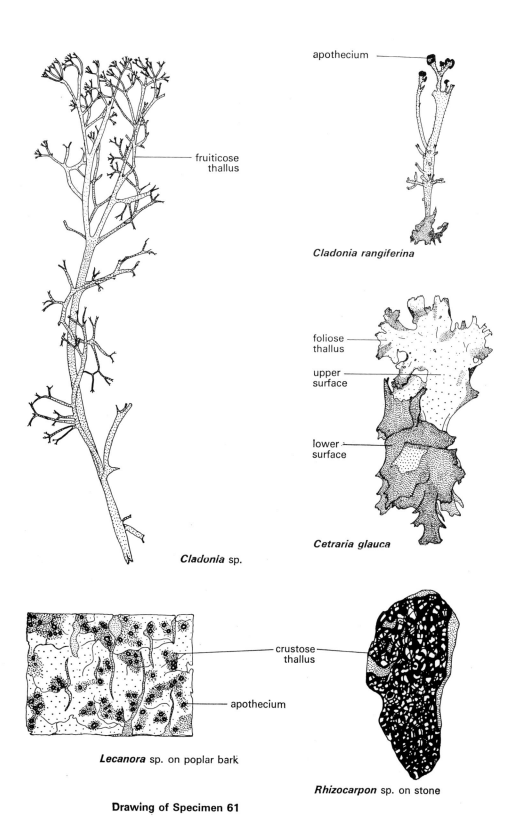

apothecium

fruiticose
thallus

Cladonia rangiferina

foliose
thallus

upper
surface

lower
surface

Cetraria glauca

Cladonia sp.

crustose
thallus

apothecium

Lecanora sp. on poplar bark

Rhizocarpon sp. on stone

Drawing of Specimen 61

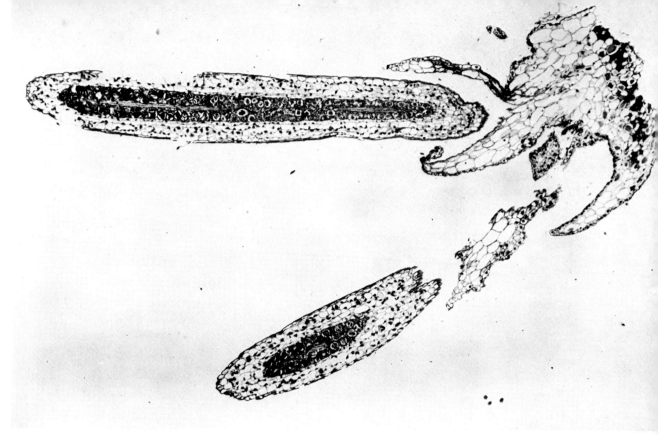

63. *Anthoceros,* sporophyte LS. Mag. ×100

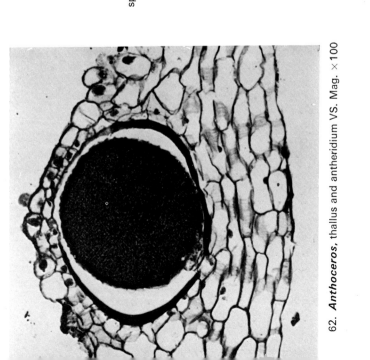

62. ***Anthoceros,*** thallus and antheridium VS. Mag. ×100

64. *Lophocolea,* gross specimen. Mag. ×10

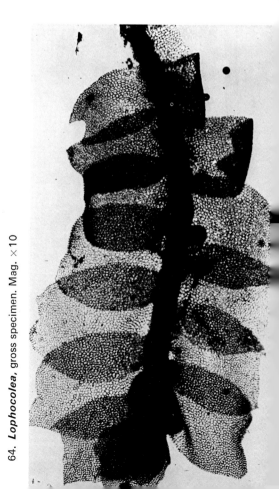

Drawing of Specimen 62

- roof cells broken open to expose mature antheridium
- roof cells
- antherozoids
- antheridium which develops endogenously
- antheridial cavity
- stalk
- single large chloroplast with starch grains
- parenchymatous cells of thallus
- small cells of lower surface
- rhizoid and mucilage mass

Drawing of Specimen 63

- mature spores
- amphithecium
- region 'A'
- developing spores
- columella
- foot
- calyptra formed from archegonial wall

DETAIL OF REGION 'A'

- epidermis with cuticle and stomata
- columella
- spore tetrads
- amphithecial cells
- pseudoelaters

Drawing of Specimen 64

- bidentate leaf
- ventral surface of stem
- leaves obliquely set in two ranks, each leaf one cell thick
- divided underleaf
- thin wall
- chloroplasts
- cytoplasm

DETAIL OF LEAF CELLS

35

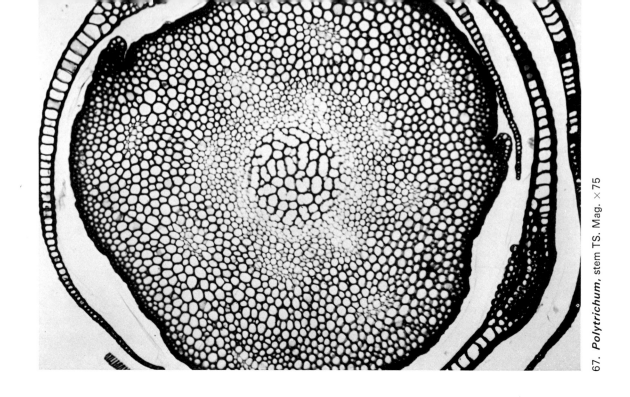

67. *Polytrichum*, stem TS. Mag. ×75

65. **Sphagnum,** stem TS. Mag. ×110

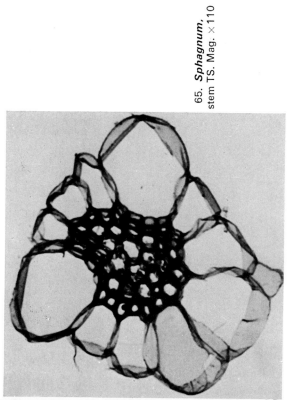

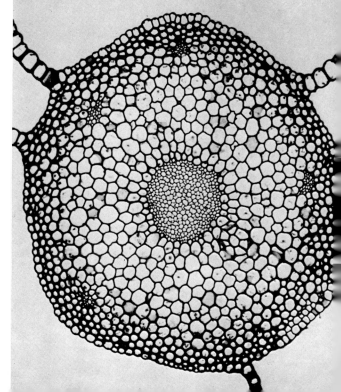

epidermis of
thick-walled cells

leaf trace
(connects with
central cylinder)

thick-walled
cells of cortex

mantle of cells
containing
starch grains

thin-walled cells
of leptome
thought to be concerned
with food conduction

large thickened cells
of hadrome
involved in
water conduction

central conducting tissue
or hadrome

leaf trace

mantle

leptome

cortex

Drawing of Specimen 67

medulla of
thin-walled cells

thicker-walled
supporting cells

cortex or hyalodermis
of dead, empty cells
which absorb water

medulla

cortex

Drawing of Specimen 65

rhizoid

small thick-walled
cells functioning
as an epidermis

chloroplasts

starch grains

region of
thicker-walled cells

'leaf' trace not
connected to axis

cortex

slightly
thicker-walled
layer of cortex

axial
cylinder

cylinder of
thin-walled cells

Drawing of Specimen 66

37

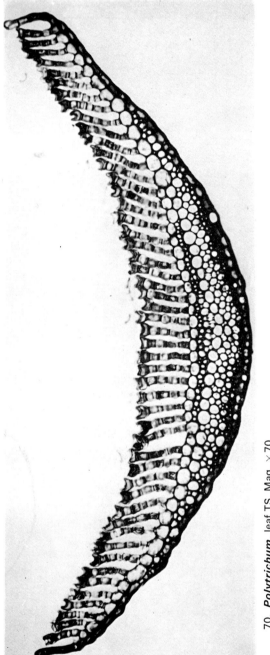

70. *Polytrichum*, leaf TS. Mag. ×70

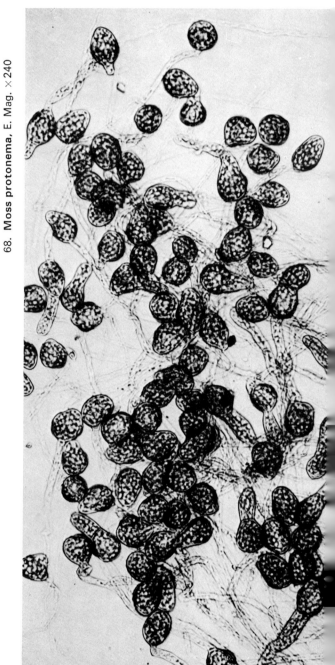

68. Moss protonema, E. Mag. ×240

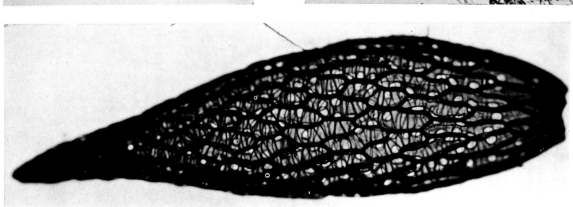

69. *Sphagnum*, leaf E. Mag. ×50

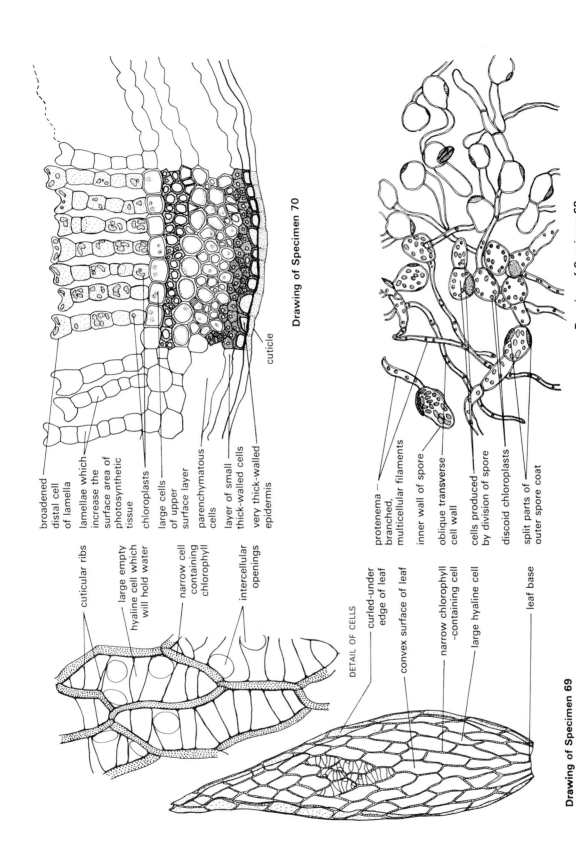

Drawing of Specimen 70

- broadened distal cell of lamella
- lamellae which increase the surface area of photosynthetic tissue
- chloroplasts
- large cells of upper surface layer
- parenchymatous cells
- layer of small thick-walled cells
- very thick-walled epidermis
- cuticle

Drawing of Specimen 68

- protenema — branched, multicellular filaments
- inner wall of spore
- oblique transverse cell wall
- cells produced by division of spore
- discoid chloroplasts
- split parts of outer spore coat

- cuticular ribs
- large empty hyaline cell which will hold water
- narrow cell containing chlorophyll
- intercellular openings

DETAIL OF CELLS

- curled-under edge of leaf
- convex surface of leaf
- narrow chlorophyll -containing cell
- large hyaline cell
- leaf base

Drawing of Specimen 69

39

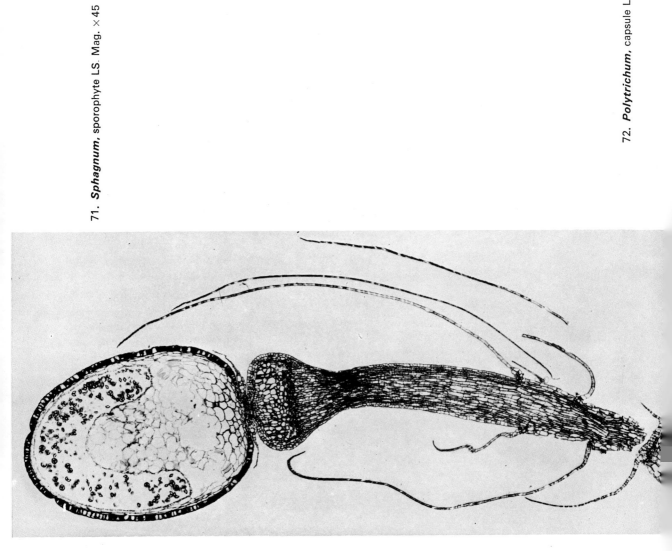

71. **Sphagnum**, sporophyte LS. Mag. ×45

72. **Polytrichum**, capsule LS. Mag. ×45

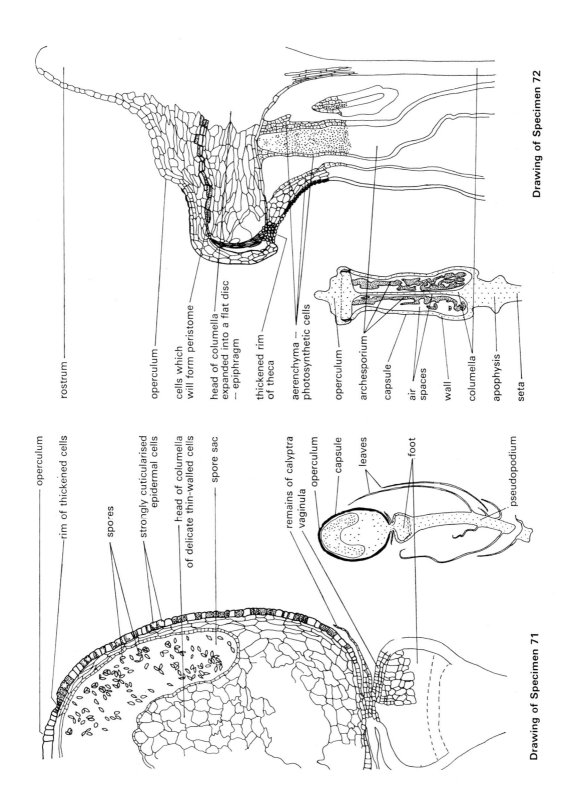

Drawing of Specimen 72

- rostrum
- operculum
- cells which will form peristome
- head of columella expanded into a flat disc — epiphragm
- thickened rim of theca
- aerenchyma — photosynthetic cells
- operculum
- archesporium
- capsule
- air spaces
- wall
- columella
- apophysis
- seta

Drawing of Specimen 71

- operculum
- rim of thickened cells
- spores
- strongly cuticularised epidermal cells
- head of columella of delicate thin-walled cells
- spore sac
- remains of calyptra vaginula
- operculum
- capsule
- leaves
- foot
- pseudopodium

73. Bryophytes, gross specimens. Mag. ×2.

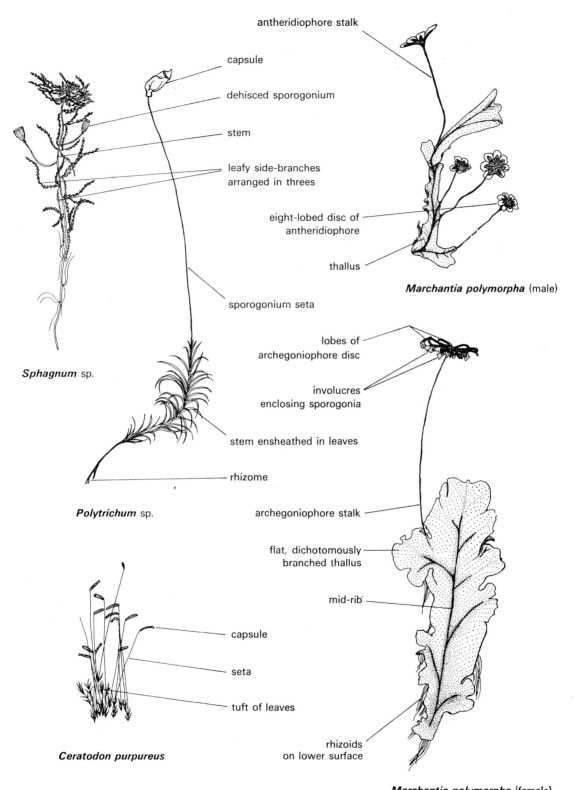

antheridiophore stalk

capsule

dehisced sporogonium

stem

leafy side-branches
arranged in threes

eight-lobed disc of
antheridiophore

thallus

Marchantia polymorpha (male)

sporogonium seta

Sphagnum sp.

lobes of
archegoniophore disc

involucres
enclosing sporogonia

stem ensheathed in leaves

rhizome

Polytrichum sp.

archegoniophore stalk

flat, dichotomously
branched thallus

mid-rib

capsule

seta

tuft of leaves

rhizoids
on lower surface

Ceratodon purpureus

Marchantia polymorpha (female)

Drawing of Specimen 73

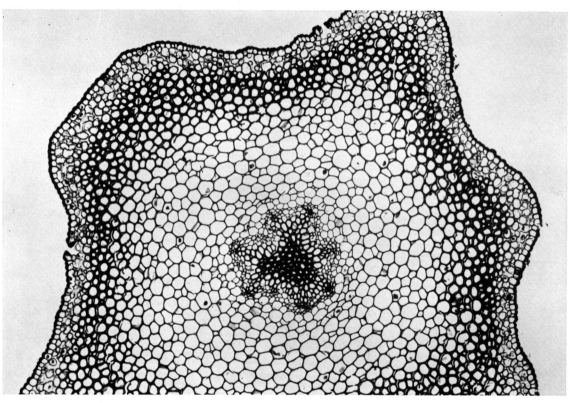

74. *Psilotum,* stem TS. Mag. ×50

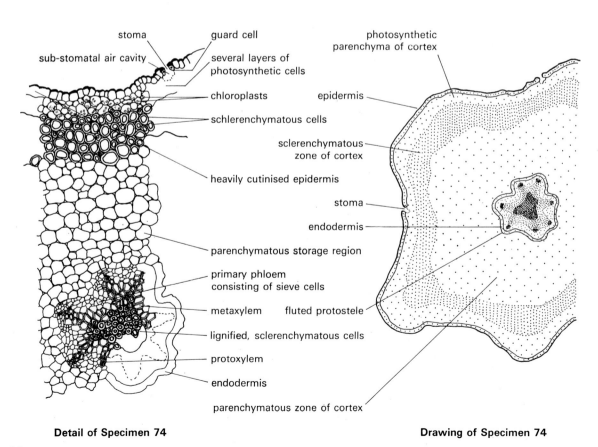

stoma

guard cell

sub-stomatal air cavity

several layers of
photosynthetic cells

chloroplasts

schlerenchymatous cells

heavily cutinised epidermis

parenchymatous storage region

primary phloem
consisting of sieve cells

metaxylem

lignified, sclerenchymatous cells

protoxylem

endodermis

Detail of Specimen 74

photosynthetic
parenchyma of cortex

epidermis

sclerenchymatous
zone of cortex

stoma

endodermis

fluted protostele

parenchymatous zone of cortex

Drawing of Specimen 74

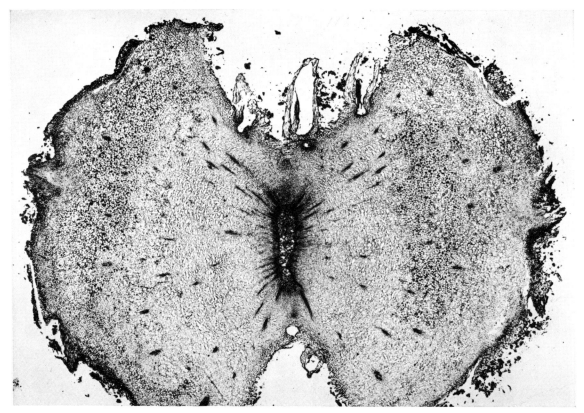

75. *Isoetes*, stem TS. Mag. ×45

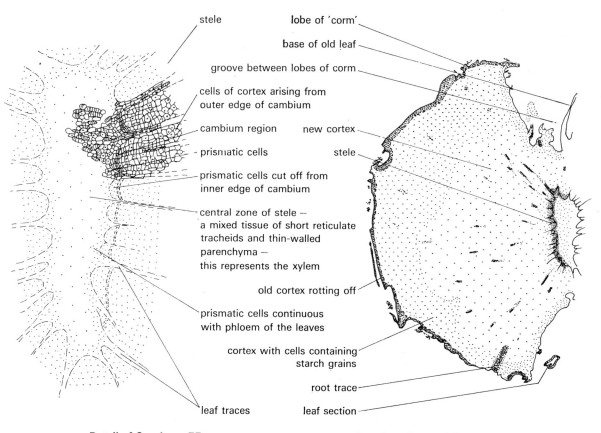

stele

lobe of 'corm'

base of old leaf

groove between lobes of corm

cells of cortex arising from
outer edge of cambium

cambium region

new cortex

prismatic cells

stele

prismatic cells cut off from
inner edge of cambium

central zone of stele —
a mixed tissue of short reticulate
tracheids and thin-walled
parenchyma —
this represents the xylem

old cortex rotting off

prismatic cells continuous
with phloem of the leaves

cortex with cells containing
starch grains

root trace

leaf section

leaf traces

Detail of Specimen 75

Drawing of part of Specimen 75

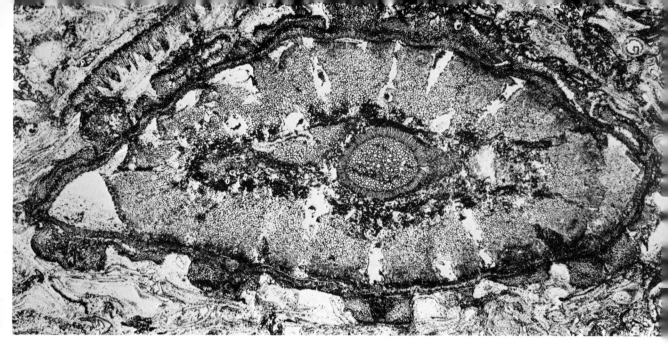

76. *Lepidodendron selaginoides,* fossil stem TS. Mag. ×20

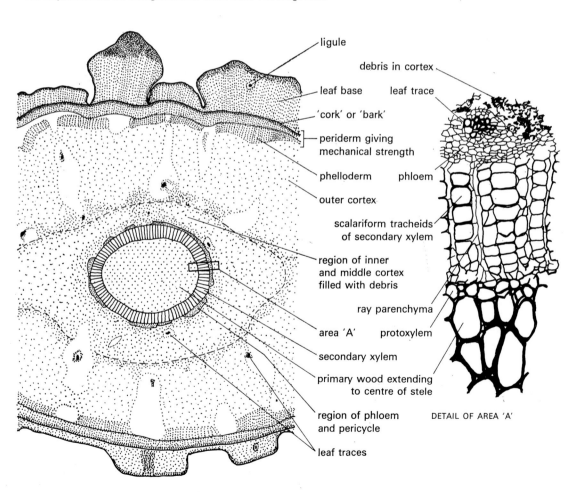

ligule

debris in cortex — leaf trace

leaf base

'cork' or 'bark'

periderm giving
mechanical strength

phelloderm — phloem

outer cortex

scalariform tracheids
of secondary xylem

region of inner
and middle cortex
filled with debris

ray parenchyma

area 'A' — protoxylem

secondary xylem

primary wood extending
to centre of stele

DETAIL OF AREA 'A'

region of phloem
and pericycle

leaf traces

Drawing of part of Specimen 76

77. *Lyginopteris,* stem TS. Mag. ×18

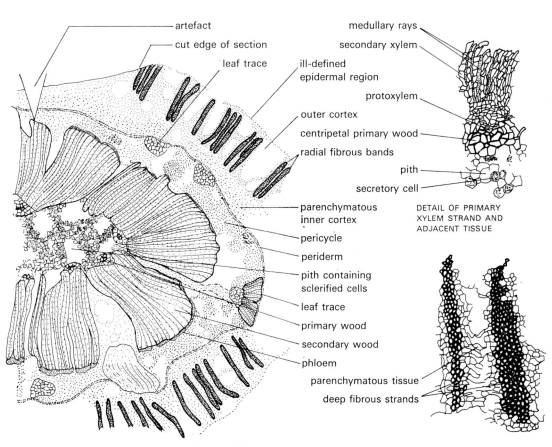

artefact

cut edge of section

leaf trace

ill-defined
epidermal region

outer cortex

radial fibrous bands

parenchymatous
inner cortex

pericycle

periderm

pith containing
sclerified cells

leaf trace

primary wood

secondary wood

phloem

medullary rays

secondary xylem

protoxylem

centripetal primary wood

pith

secretory cell

DETAIL OF PRIMARY
XYLEM STRAND AND
ADJACENT TISSUE

parenchymatous tissue

deep fibrous strands

Drawing of part of Specimen 77

DETAIL OF OUTER CORTEX

47

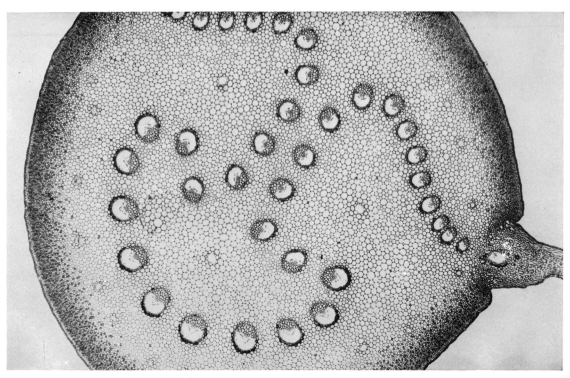

78. *Cycas,* rachis TS. Mag. ×45

79. *Cordaites,* fossil stem TS. Mag. ×50

48

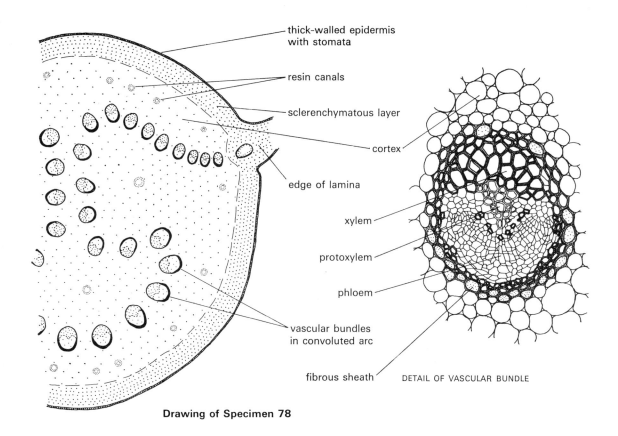

thick-walled epidermis
with stomata

resin canals

sclerenchymatous layer

cortex

edge of lamina

xylem

protoxylem

phloem

vascular bundles
in convoluted arc

fibrous sheath

DETAIL OF VASCULAR BUNDLE

Drawing of Specimen 78

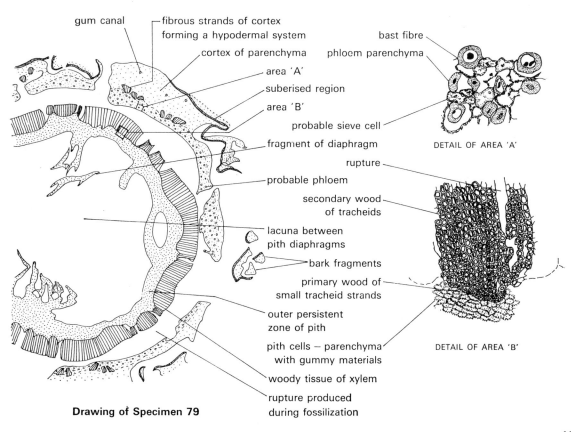

gum canal

fibrous strands of cortex
forming a hypodermal system

cortex of parenchyma

area 'A'

suberised region

area 'B'

fragment of diaphragm

probable phloem

lacuna between
pith diaphragms

bark fragments

primary wood of
small tracheid strands

outer persistent
zone of pith

pith cells — parenchyma
with gummy materials

woody tissue of xylem

rupture produced
during fossilization

bast fibre

phloem parenchyma

probable sieve cell

DETAIL OF AREA 'A'

rupture

secondary wood
of tracheids

DETAIL OF AREA 'B'

Drawing of Specimen 79

49

80 **Pteridophytes,** gross specimens. Mag. ×2

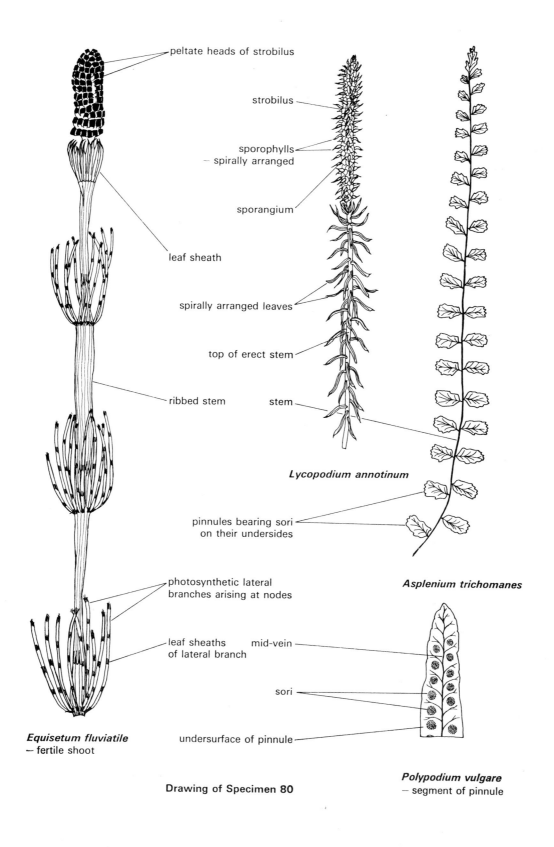

peltate heads of strobilus

strobilus

sporophylls –
spirally arranged

sporangium

leaf sheath

spirally arranged leaves

top of erect stem

ribbed stem

stem

Lycopodium annotinum

pinnules bearing sori
on their undersides

Asplenium trichomanes

photosynthetic lateral
branches arising at nodes

leaf sheaths
of lateral branch

mid-vein

sori

undersurface of pinnule

Equisetum fluviatile
– fertile shoot

Drawing of Specimen 80

Polypodium vulgare
– segment of pinnule

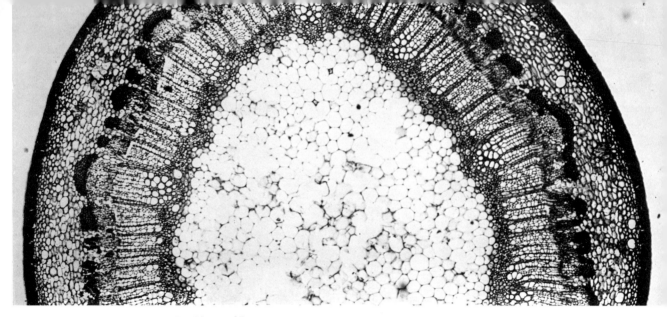

81. *Liriodendron,* stem TS. Mag. ×25

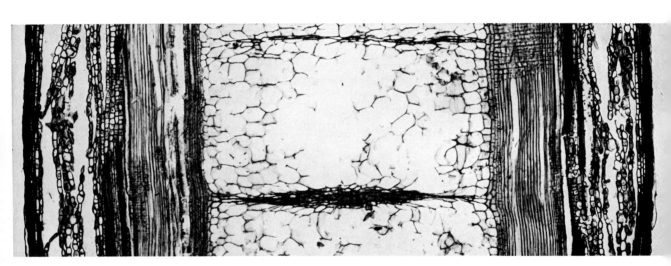

82. *Liriodendron,* stem RLS. Mag. ×25

83. *Liriodendron,* stem TLS. Mag. ×25

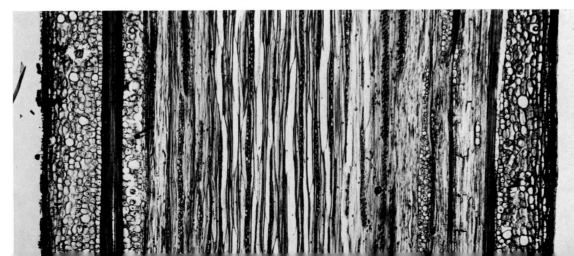

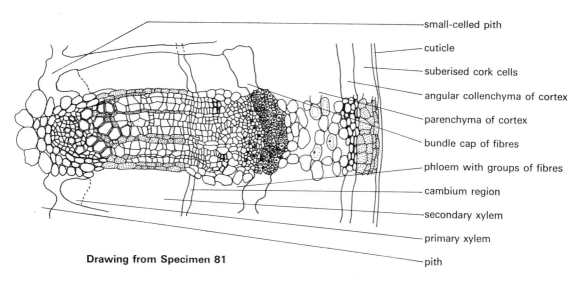

— small-celled pith
— cuticle
— suberised cork cells
— angular collenchyma of cortex
— parenchyma of cortex
— bundle cap of fibres
— phloem with groups of fibres
— cambium region
— secondary xylem
— primary xylem
— pith

Drawing from Specimen 81

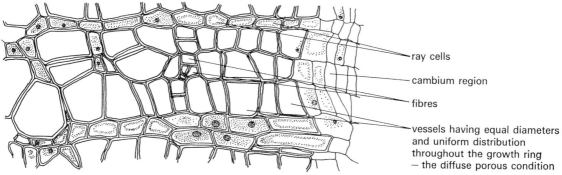

— ray cells
— cambium region
— fibres
— vessels having equal diameters and uniform distribution throughout the growth ring — the diffuse porous condition

Detail of wood of Specimen 81

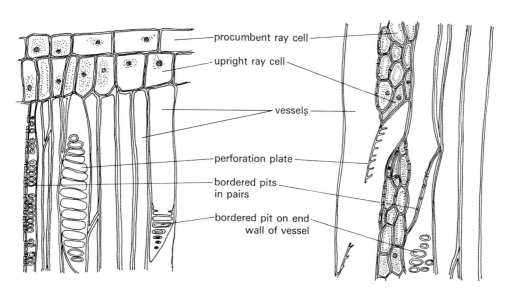

procumbent ray cell
upright ray cell
vessels
perforation plate
bordered pits in pairs
bordered pit on end wall of vessel

Detail of wood of Specimen 82

Detail of wood of Specimen 83

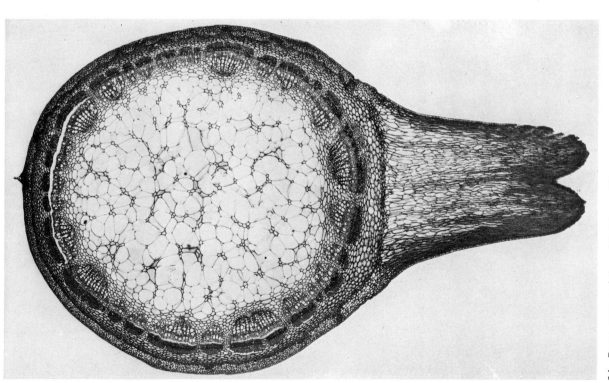

85. *Cytisus,* stem TS. Mag. ×75

84. *Rosa,* stem and thorn TS. Mag. ×30

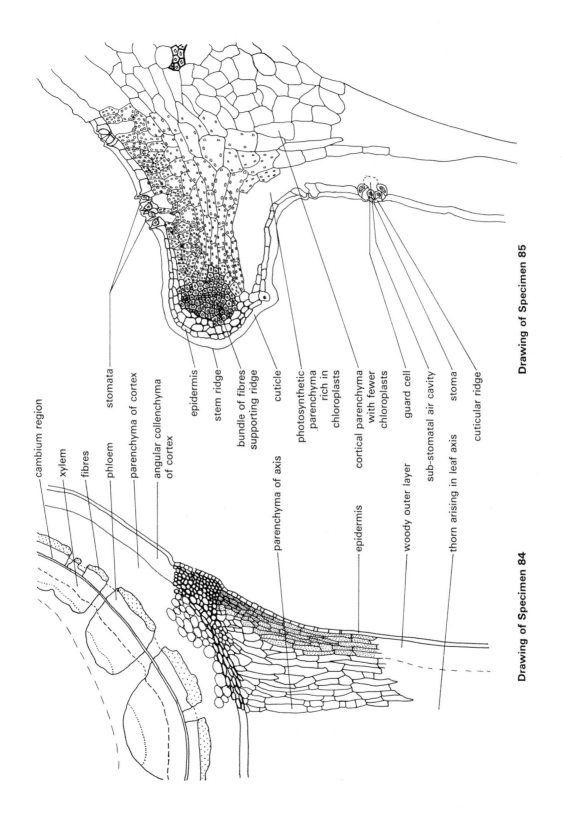

cambium region

xylem

fibres

phloem

stomata

parenchyma of cortex

angular collenchyma
of cortex

epidermis

stem ridge

bundle of fibres
supporting ridge

cuticle

photosynthetic
parenchyma
rich in
chloroplasts

cortical parenchyma
with fewer
chloroplasts

guard cell

sub-stomatal air cavity

stoma

cuticular ridge

parenchyma of axis

epidermis

woody outer layer

thorn arising in leaf axis

Drawing of Specimen 85

Drawing of Specimen 84

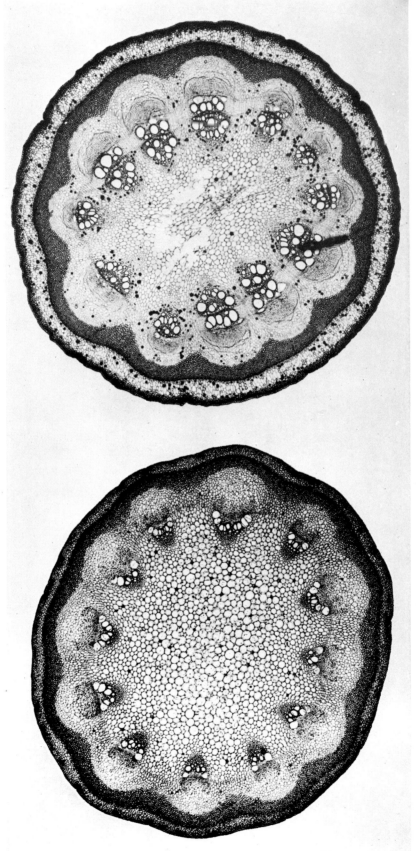

87. *Aristolochia*, two year stem TS. Mag. ×30

86. *Aristolochia*, one year stem TS. Mag. ×30

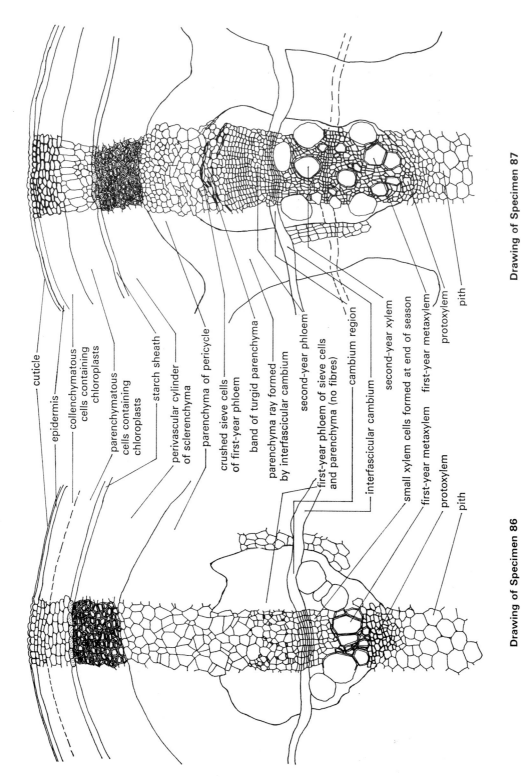

cuticle

epidermis

collenchymatous
cells containing
chloroplasts

parenchymatous
cells containing
chloroplasts

starch sheath

perivascular cylinder
of sclerenchyma

parenchyma of pericycle

crushed sieve cells
of first-year phloem

band of turgid parenchyma

parenchyma ray formed
by interfascicular cambium

second-year phloem

first-year phloem of sieve cells
and parenchyma (no fibres)

cambium region

interfascicular cambium

second-year xylem

small xylem cells formed at end of season

first-year metaxylem

first-year metaxylem

protoxylem

protoxylem

pith

pith

Drawing of Specimen 87

Drawing of Specimen 86

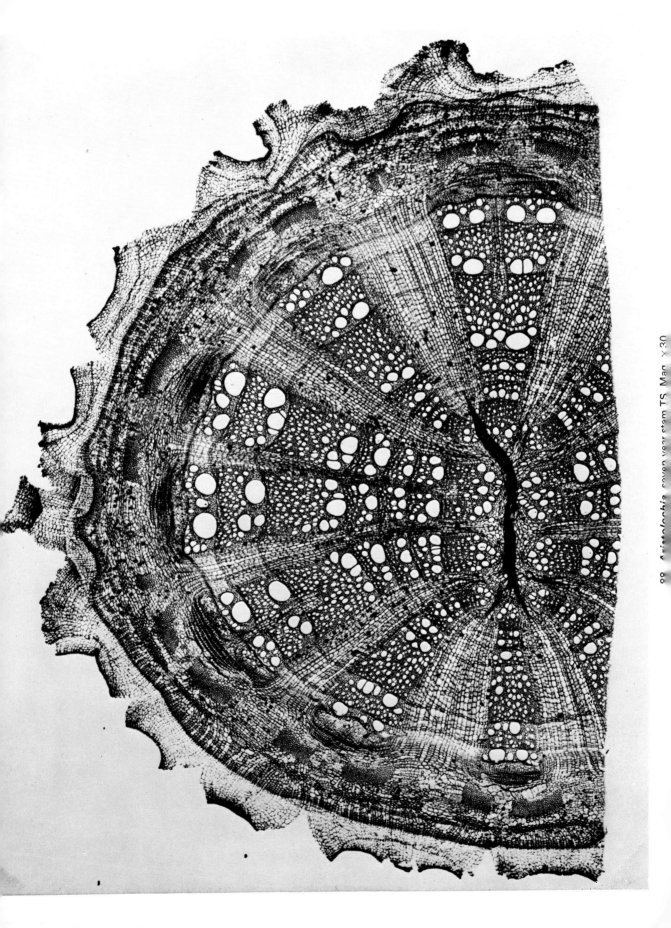

98 *Aristolochia*, seven year stem T.S. Mag. ×30

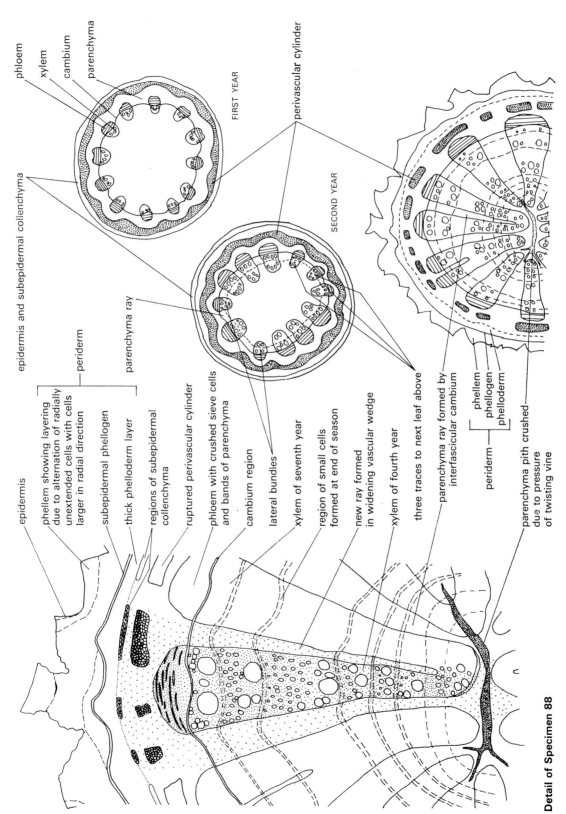

phloem

xylem

cambium

parenchyma

epidermis and subepidermal collenchyma

FIRST YEAR

perivascular cylinder

SECOND YEAR

SEVENTH YEAR

phellem
phellogen
phelloderm

periderm

parenchyma ray

parenchyma ray formed by
interfascicular cambium

parenchyma pith crushed
due to pressure
of twisting vine

epidermis

phellem showing layering
due to alternation of radially
unextended cells with cells
larger in radial direction

subepidermal phellogen

thick phelloderm layer

regions of subepidermal
collenchyma

ruptured perivascular cylinder

phloem with crushed sieve cells
and bands of parenchyma

cambium region

lateral bundles

xylem of seventh year

region of small cells
formed at end of season

new ray formed
in widening vascular wedge

xylem of fourth year

three traces to next leaf above

periderm

Detail of Specimen 88

Drawings of Specimens 86, 87 and 88 to show development of secondary tissues

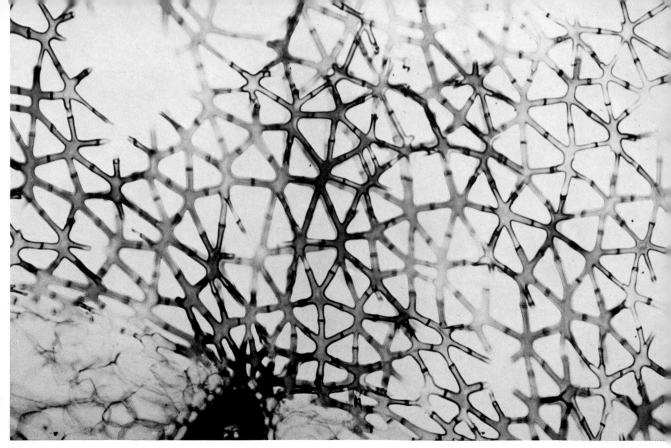

89. *Juncus,* stem TS. Mag. ×350

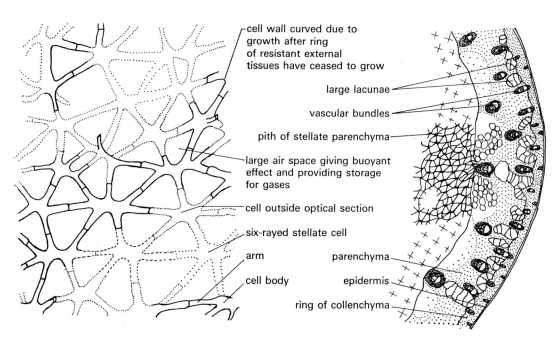

cell wall curved due to
growth after ring
of resistant external
tissues have ceased to grow

large lacunae

vascular bundles

pith of stellate parenchyma

large air space giving buoyant
effect and providing storage
for gases

cell outside optical section

six-rayed stellate cell

arm

cell body

parenchyma

epidermis

ring of collenchyma

Drawing of Specimen 89

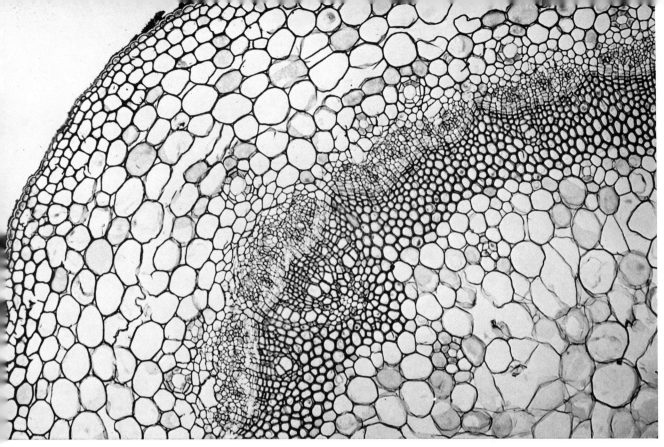

90. *Hedera,* stem TS. Mag. ×240

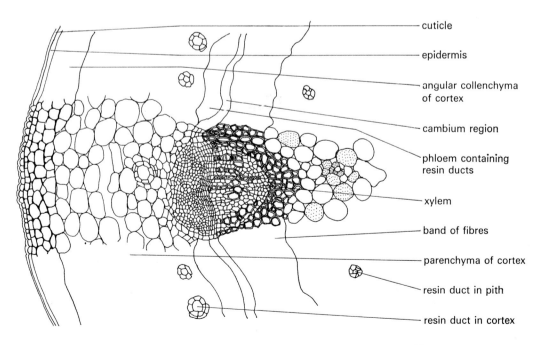

cuticle

epidermis

angular collenchyma
of cortex

cambium region

phloem containing
resin ducts

xylem

band of fibres

parenchyma of cortex

resin duct in pith

resin duct in cortex

Drawing of Specimen 90

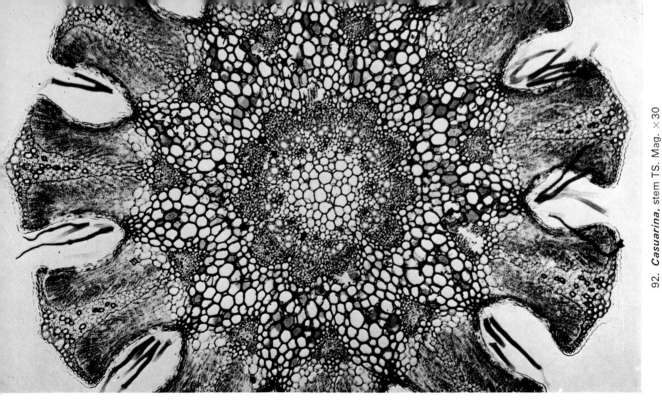

92. *Casuarina*, stem TS. Mag. ×30

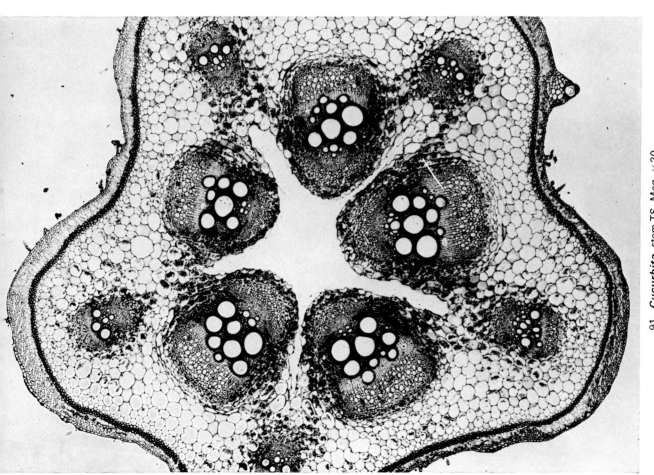

91. *Cucurbita*, stem TS. Mag. ×30

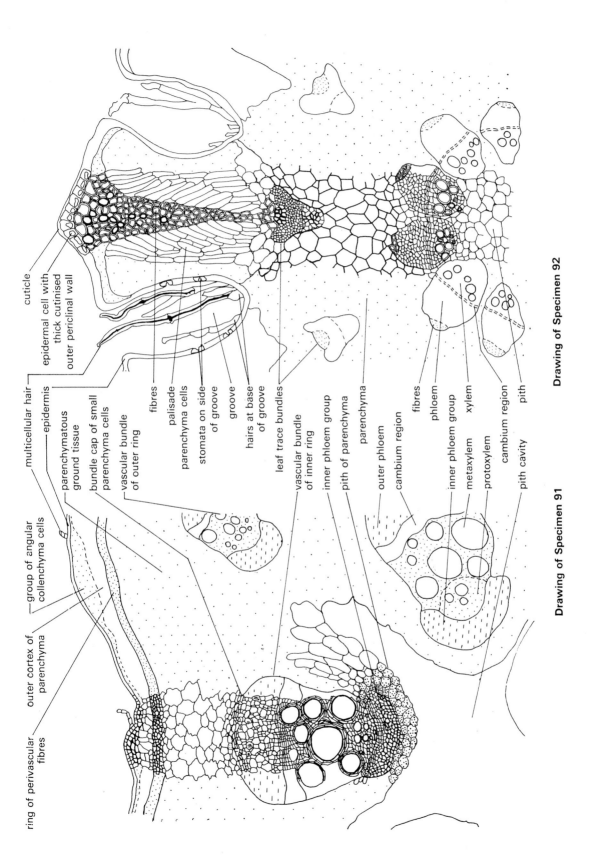

cuticle

epidermal cell with
thick cutinised
outer periclinal wall

multicellular hair

epidermis

parenchymatous
ground tissue

bundle cap of small
parenchyma cells

vascular bundle
of outer ring

fibres

palisade
parenchyma cells

stomata on side
of groove

groove

hairs at base
of groove

leaf trace bundles

vascular bundle
of inner ring

inner phloem group

pith of parenchyma

parenchyma

outer phloem

cambium region

fibres

phloem

inner phloem group

metaxylem

xylem

protoxylem

cambium region

pith

pith cavity

ring of perivascular
fibres

outer cortex of
parenchyma

group of angular
collenchyma cells

Drawing of Specimen 92

Drawing of Specimen 91

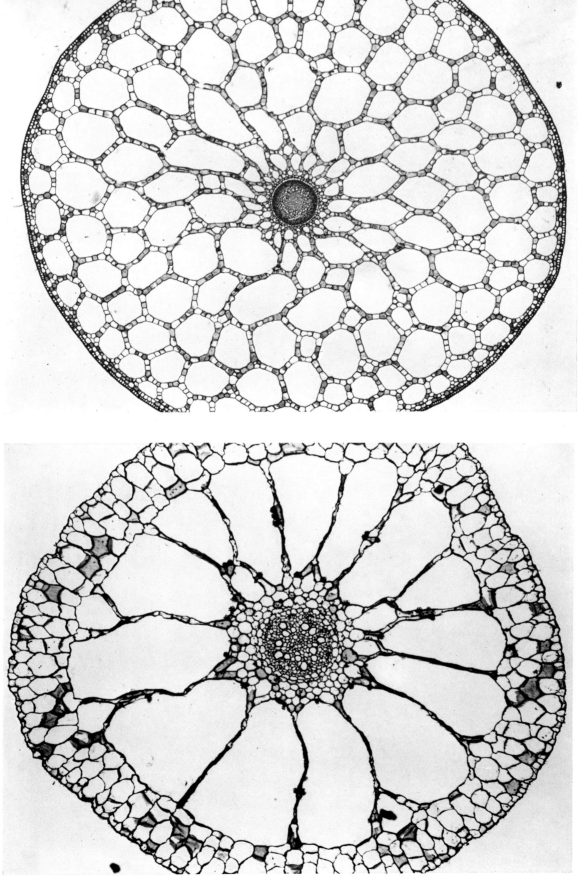

94. *Hippuris*, stem TS. Mag. × 30

93. *Myriophyllum*, stem TS. Mag. × 80

Drawing of part of Specimen 94

epidermis with cuticle

outer cortex of parenchyma

epidermis with thin cuticle

middle cortex of parenchyma
with large intercellular lacunae

outer cortex of three layers
of parenchyma cells

lacunae containing air

large air space
(lacuna)

radial strand
of parenchyma

middle cortex

crystalline inclusion

small air space

pith

phloem

inner cortex

inner cortex of compact
parenchyma cells

endodermis

xylem

pith

endodermis

phloem

xylem

Drawing of part of Specimen 93

65

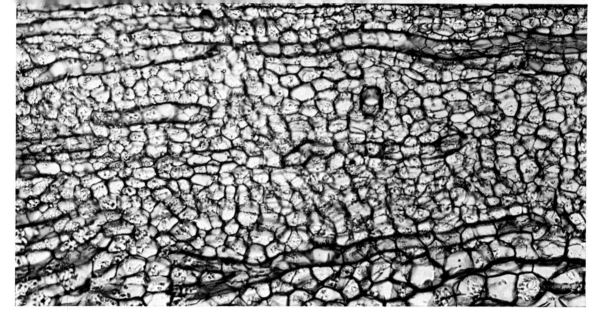

95. *Euphorbia,* stem LS. Mag. ×255

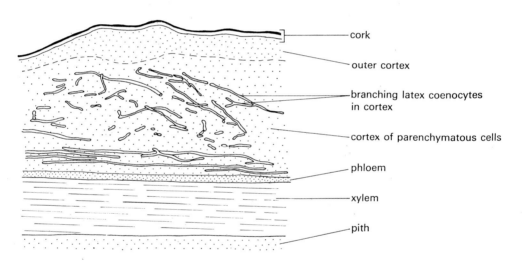

cork

outer cortex

branching latex coenocytes
in cortex

cortex of parenchymatous cells

phloem

xylem

pith

LOW-POWER PLAN TO SHOW POSITION OF SPECIMEN 95

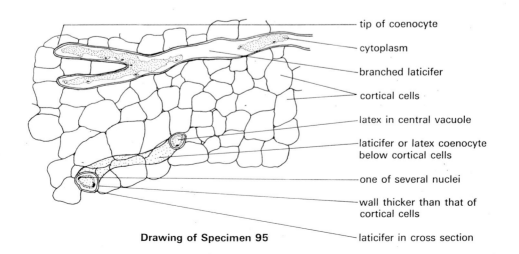

tip of coenocyte

cytoplasm

branched laticifer

cortical cells

latex in central vacuole

laticifer or latex coenocyte
below cortical cells

one of several nuclei

wall thicker than that of
cortical cells

Drawing of Specimen 95

laticifer in cross section

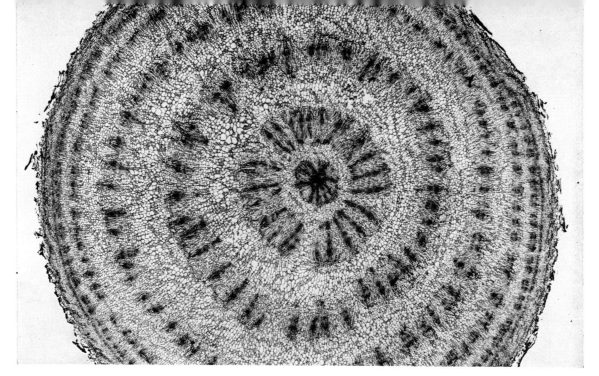

96. **Beta,** root TS. Mag. ×25

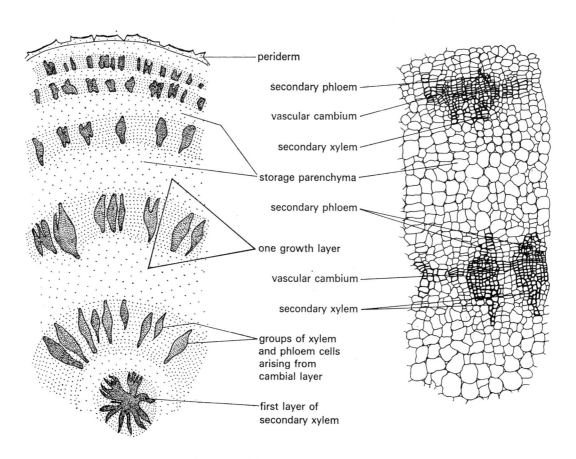

periderm

secondary phloem

vascular cambium

secondary xylem

storage parenchyma

secondary phloem

one growth layer

vascular cambium

secondary xylem

groups of xylem
and phloem cells
arising from
cambial layer

first layer of
secondary xylem

Drawing of Specimen 96   DETAIL OF SPECIMEN 96

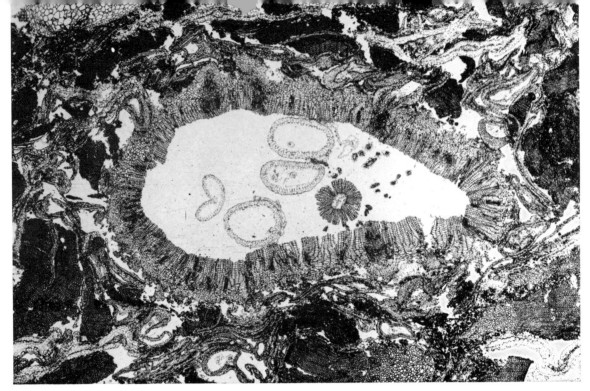

97. *Lepidodendron*, fossil root TS. Mag. ×18

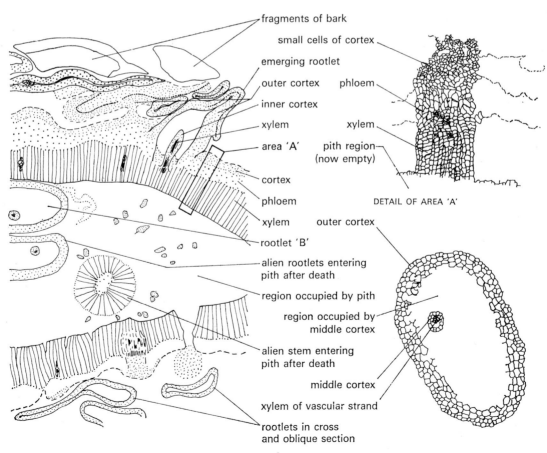

fragments of bark

small cells of cortex

emerging rootlet

outer cortex — phloem

inner cortex

xylem

area 'A' — xylem

pith region
(now empty)

cortex

phloem

xylem

rootlet 'B'

DETAIL OF AREA 'A'

alien rootlets entering
pith after death

outer cortex

region occupied by pith

region occupied by
middle cortex

alien stem entering
pith after death

middle cortex

xylem of vascular strand

rootlets in cross
and oblique section

68   **Drawing of part of Specimen 97**   DETAIL OF ROOTLET 'B'

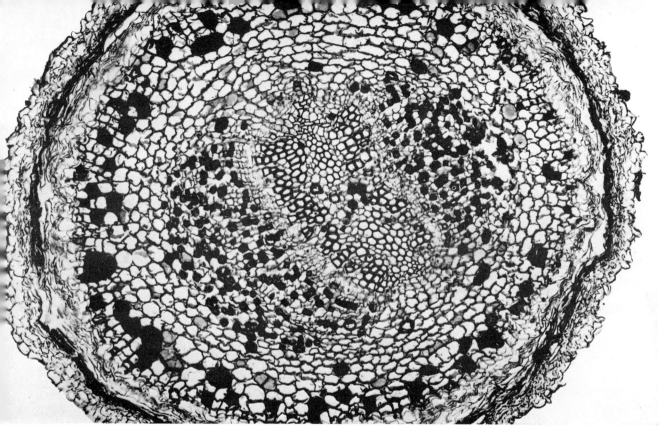

98. *Zamia,* root TS. Mag. ×20

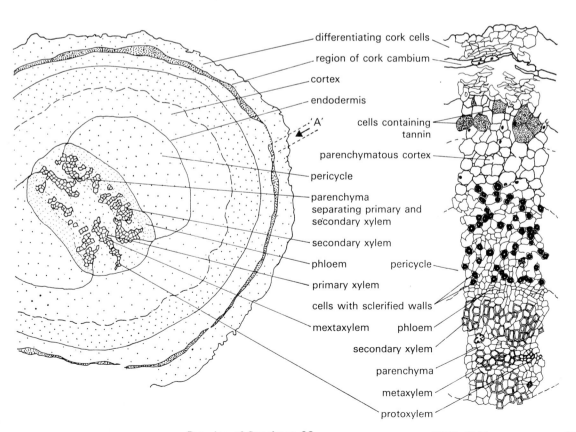

differentiating cork cells

region of cork cambium

cortex

endodermis

'A'

cells containing tannin

parenchymatous cortex

pericycle

parenchyma separating primary and secondary xylem

secondary xylem

phloem   pericycle

primary xylem

cells with sclerified walls

mextaxylem   phloem

secondary xylem

parenchyma

metaxylem

protoxylem

Drawing of Specimen 98   DETAIL AT 'A'   69

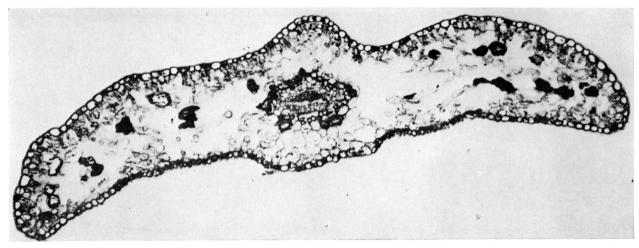

99. *Taxus*, leaf TS. Mag. ×35

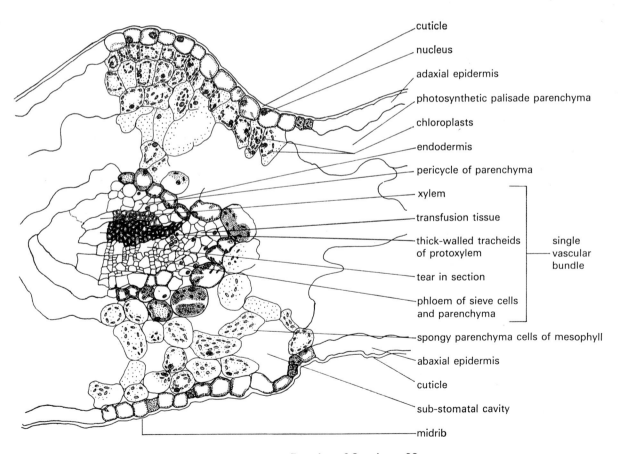

cuticle

nucleus

adaxial epidermis

photosynthetic palisade parenchyma

chloroplasts

endodermis

pericycle of parenchyma

xylem

transfusion tissue

thick-walled tracheids
of protoxylem

tear in section

phloem of sieve cells
and parenchyma

single
vascular
bundle

spongy parenchyma cells of mesophyll

abaxial epidermis

cuticle

sub-stomatal cavity

midrib

Drawing of Specimen 99

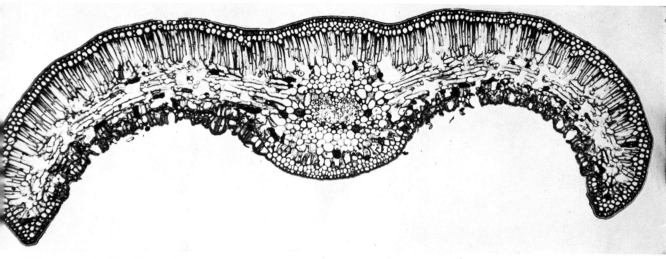

100. *Cycas,* leaf TS. Mag. ×35

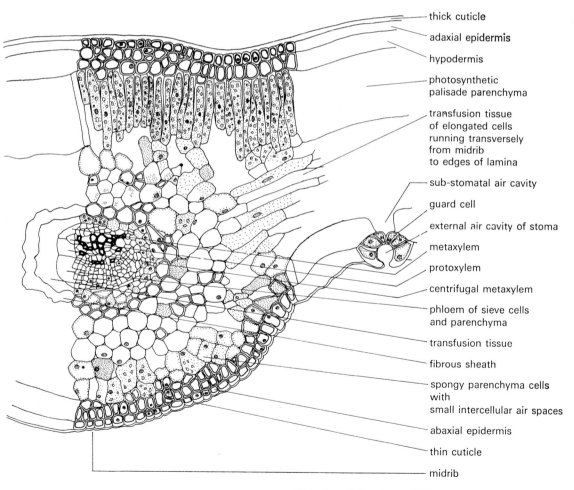

thick cuticle

adaxial epidermis

hypodermis

photosynthetic
palisade parenchyma

transfusion tissue
of elongated cells
running transversely
from midrib
to edges of lamina

sub-stomatal air cavity

guard cell

external air cavity of stoma

metaxylem

protoxylem

centrifugal metaxylem

phloem of sieve cells
and parenchyma

transfusion tissue

fibrous sheath

spongy parenchyma cells
with
small intercellular air spaces

abaxial epidermis

thin cuticle

midrib

Drawing of Specimen 100

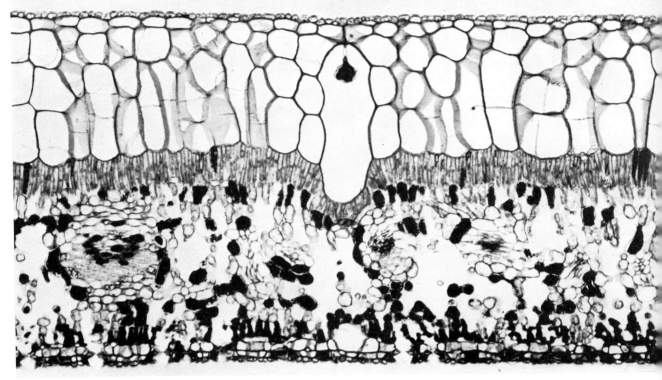

101. *Ficus,* leaf TS. Mag. ×200

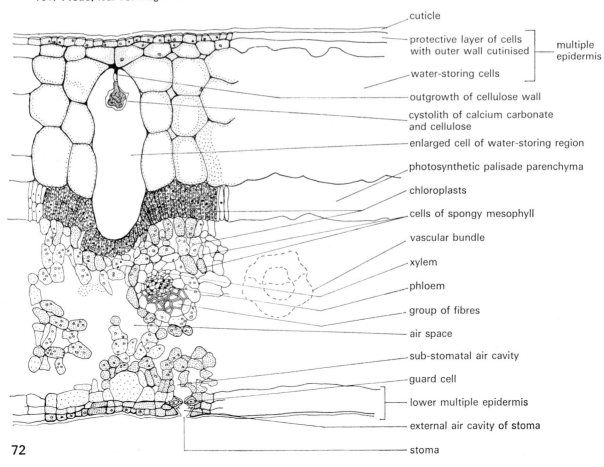

cuticle

protective layer of cells
with outer wall cutinised

multiple
epidermis

water-storing cells

outgrowth of cellulose wall

cystolith of calcium carbonate
and cellulose

enlarged cell of water-storing region

photosynthetic palisade parenchyma

chloroplasts

cells of spongy mesophyll

vascular bundle

xylem

phloem

group of fibres

air space

sub-stomatal air cavity

guard cell

lower multiple epidermis

external air cavity of stoma

stoma

72

Drawing of Specimen 101

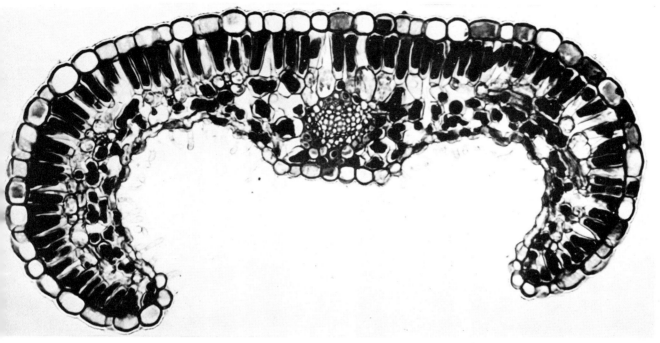

102. *Erica,* leaf TS. Mag. ×40

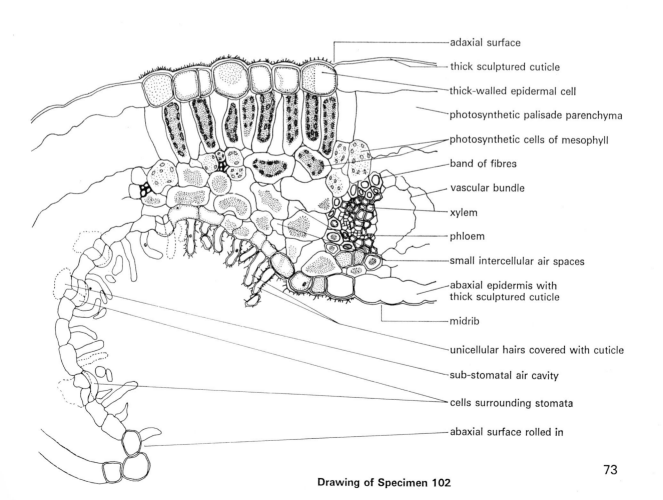

adaxial surface

thick sculptured cuticle

thick-walled epidermal cell

photosynthetic palisade parenchyma

photosynthetic cells of mesophyll

band of fibres

vascular bundle

xylem

phloem

small intercellular air spaces

abaxial epidermis with
thick sculptured cuticle

midrib

unicellular hairs covered with cuticle

sub-stomatal air cavity

cells surrounding stomata

abaxial surface rolled in

Drawing of Specimen 102

73

103. *Hakea,* leaf TS. Mag. ×35

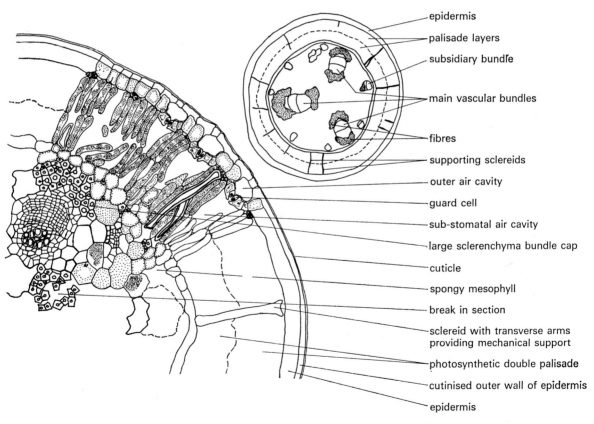

epidermis

palisade layers

subsidiary bundle

main vascular bundles

fibres

supporting sclereids

outer air cavity

guard cell

sub-stomatal air cavity

large sclerenchyma bundle cap

cuticle

spongy mesophyll

break in section

sclereid with transverse arms
providing mechanical support

photosynthetic double palisade

cutinised outer wall of epidermis

epidermis

Drawing of Specimen 103

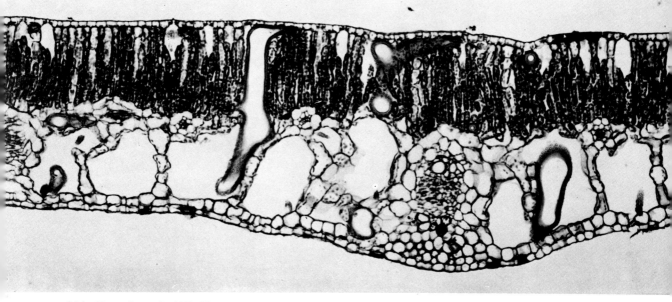

104. *Nymphaea*, leaf TS. Mag. ×175

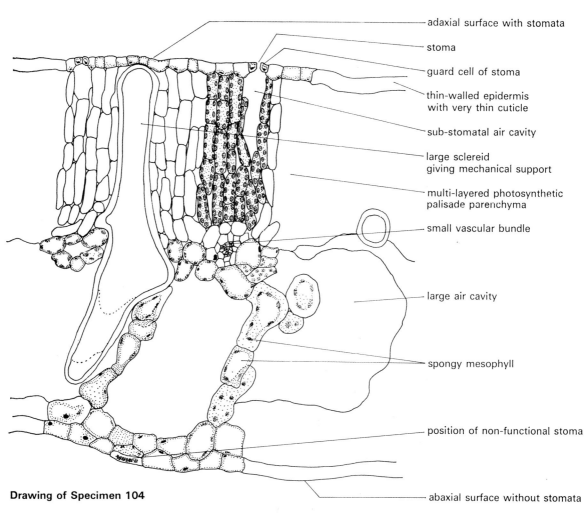

- adaxial surface with stomata
- stoma
- guard cell of stoma
- thin-walled epidermis with very thin cuticle
- sub-stomatal air cavity
- large sclereid giving mechanical support
- multi-layered photosynthetic palisade parenchyma
- small vascular bundle
- large air cavity
- spongy mesophyll
- position of non-functional stoma
- abaxial surface without stomata

Drawing of Specimen 104

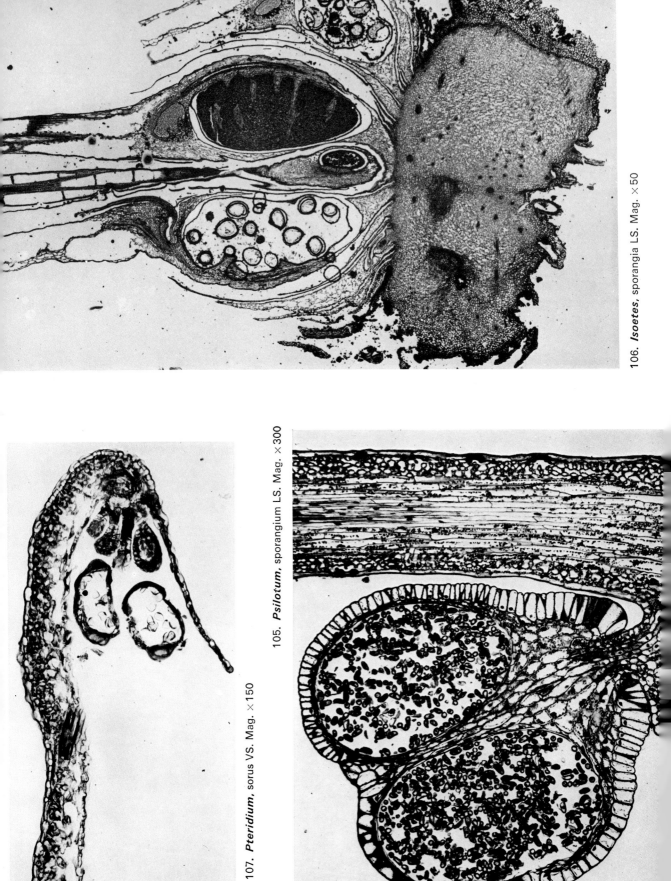

106. **Isoetes**, sporangia LS. Mag. ×50

107. **Pteridium**, sorus VS. Mag. ×150

105. **Psilotum**, sporangium LS. Mag. ×300

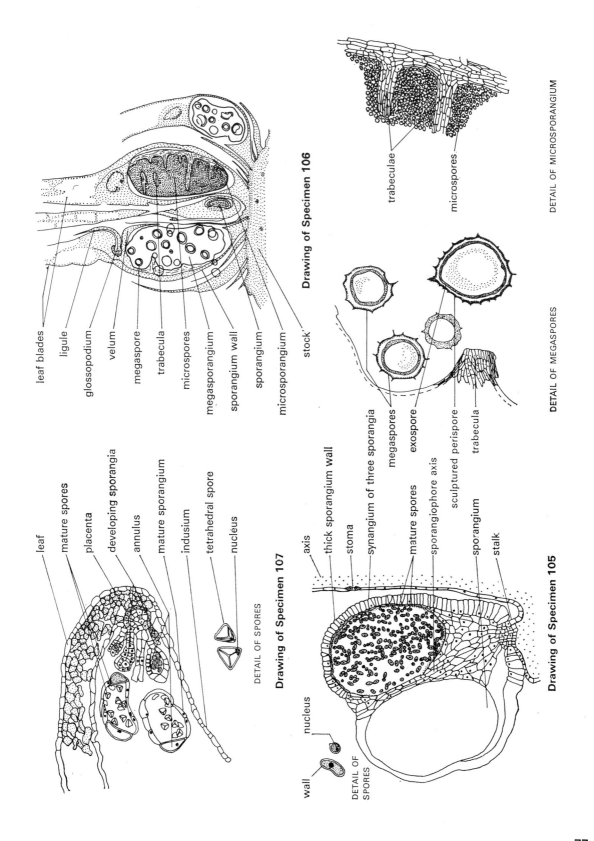

leaf

mature spores

placenta

developing **sporangia**

annulus

mature sporangium

indusium

tetrahedral spore

nucleus

DETAIL OF SPORES

Drawing of Specimen 107

leaf blades

ligule

glossopodium

velum

megaspore

trabecula

microspores

megasporangium

sporangium wall

sporangium

microsporangium

stock

Drawing of Specimen 106

trabeculae

microspores

DETAIL OF MICROSPORANGIUM

axis

thick sporangium wall

stoma

synangium of three sporangia

mature spores

sporangiophore axis

sporangium

stalk

wall

nucleus

DETAIL OF SPORES

Drawing of Specimen 105

megaspores

exospore

sculptured perispore

trabecula

DETAIL OF MEGASPORES

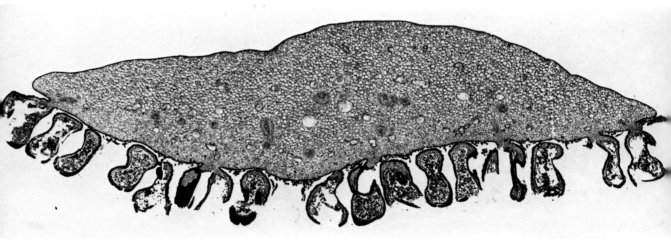

108. *Cycas,* microsporangia VS. Mag. ×45

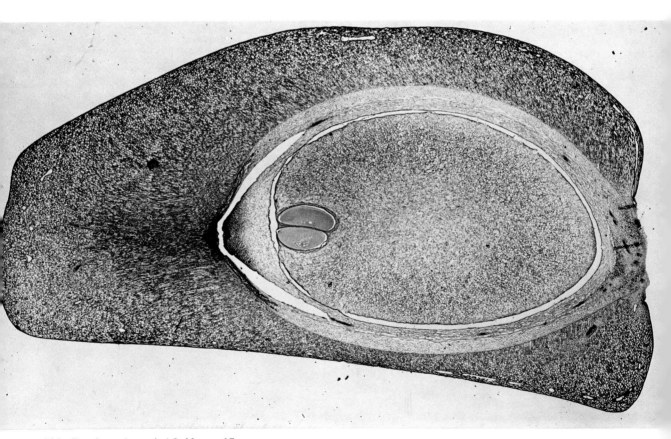

109. *Zamia,* archegonia LS. Mag. ×15

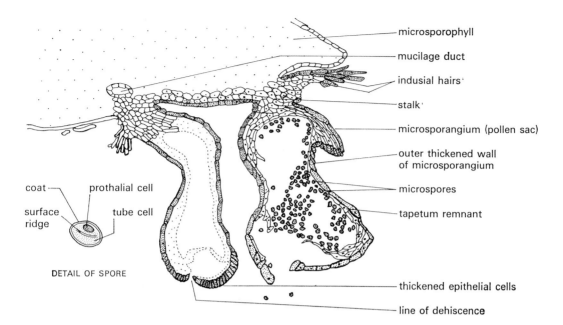

microsporophyll

mucilage duct

indusial hairs·

stalk·

microsporangium (pollen sac)

outer thickened wall
of microsporangium

microspores

tapetum remnant

thickened epithelial cells

line of dehiscence

coat

prothalial cell

surface
ridge

tube cell

DETAIL OF SPORE

Drawing of part of Specimen 108

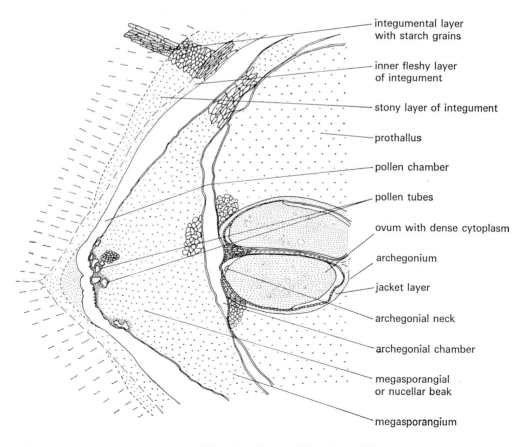

integumental layer
with starch grains

inner fleshy layer
of integument

stony layer of integument

prothallus

pollen chamber

pollen tubes

ovum with dense cytoplasm

archegonium

jacket layer

archegonial neck

archegonial chamber

megasporangial
or nucellar beak

megasporangium

Drawing of part of Specimen 109

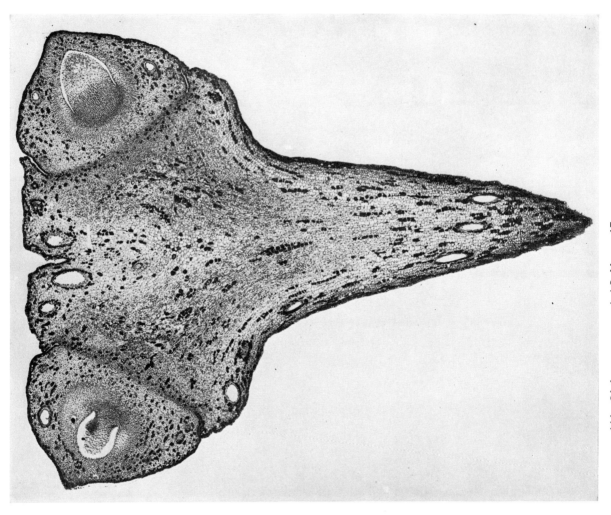

111. *Ginkgo,* young ovule LS. Mag. ×17

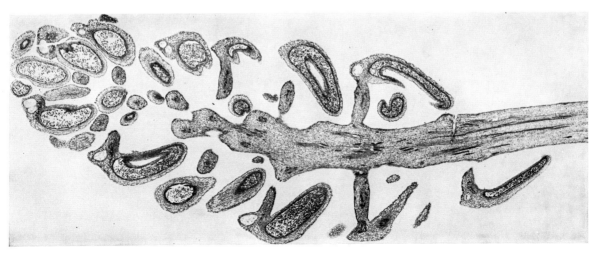

110. *Ginkgo,* male cone LS. Mag. ×20

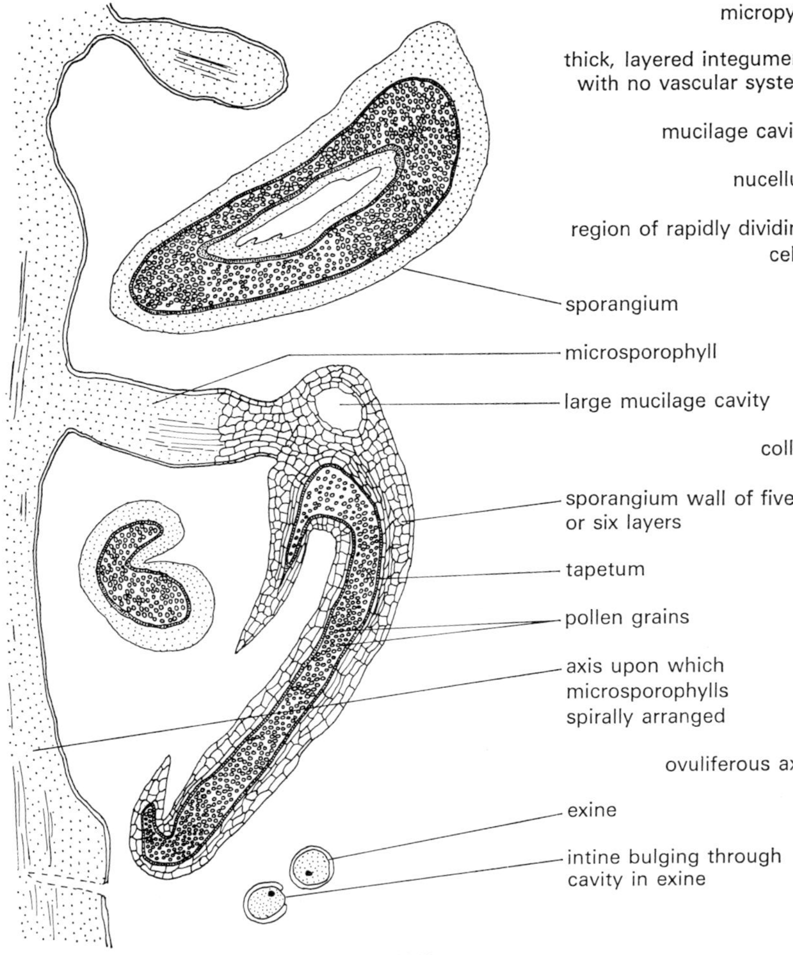

position of formation of
micropyle

thick, layered integument
with no vascular system

mucilage cavity

nucellus

region of rapidly dividing
cells

sporangium

microsporophyll

large mucilage cavity

collar

sporangium wall of five
or six layers

tapetum

pollen grains

axis upon which
microsporophylls
spirally arranged

ovuliferous axis

exine

intine bulging through
cavity in exine

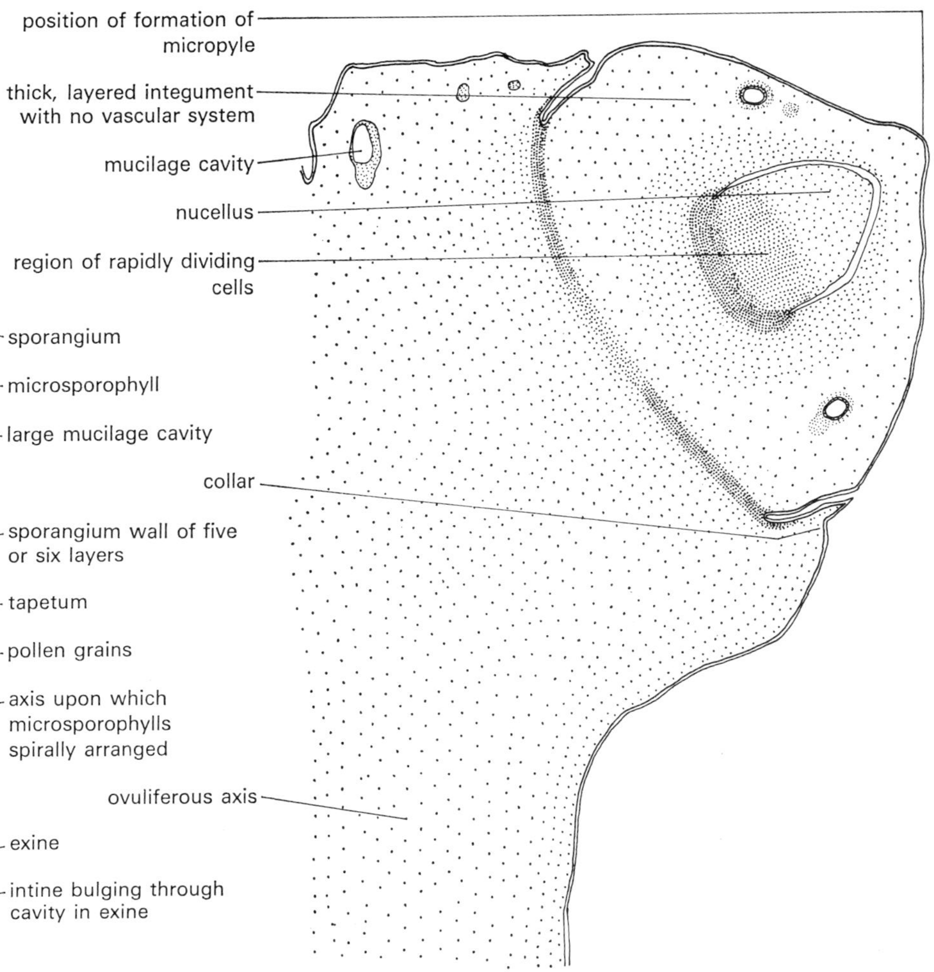

Drawing of Specimen 111

DETAIL OF POLLEN GRAINS

Drawing of Specimen 110

81

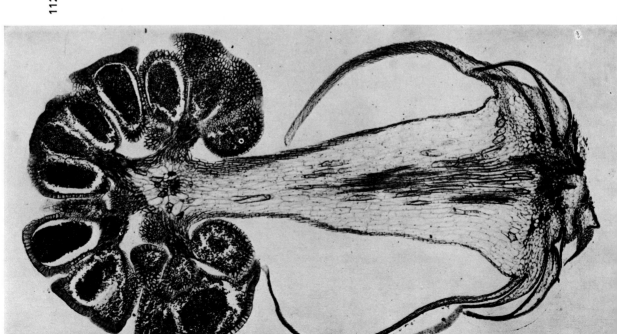

112. **Taxus**, male cone LS.
Mag. ×12

113. **Taxus**, female cone LS.
Mag. ×14

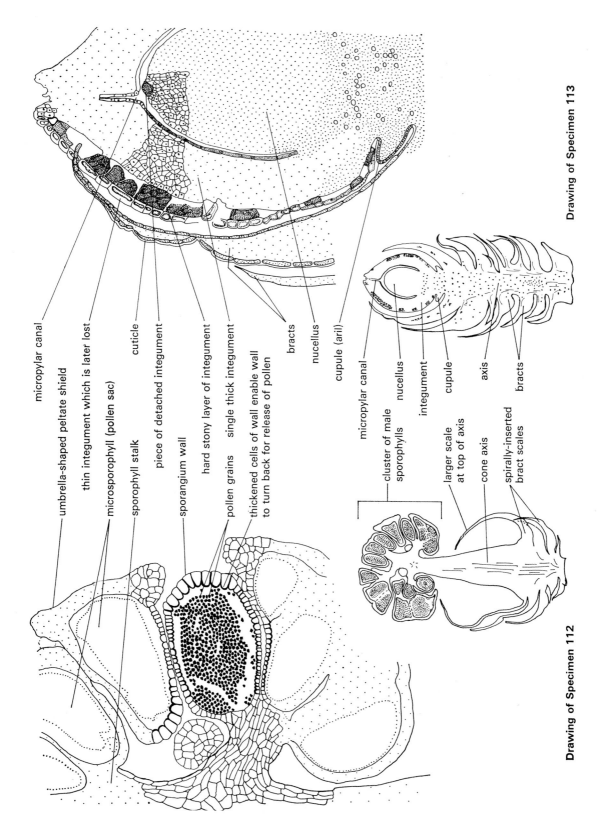

micropylar canal

umbrella-shaped peltate shield

thin integument which is later lost

microsporophyll (pollen sac)

cuticle

sporophyll stalk

piece of detached integument

sporangium wall

hard stony layer of integument

pollen grains

single thick integument

thickened cells of wall enable wall
to turn back for release of pollen

bracts

nucellus

cupule (aril)

micropylar canal

cluster of male
sporophylls

nucellus

integument

cupule

larger scale
at top of axis

cone axis

spirally-inserted
bract scales

axis

bracts

Drawing of Specimen 113

Drawing of Specimen 112

114. **Gymnosperms,** gross specimens. Mag. ×2

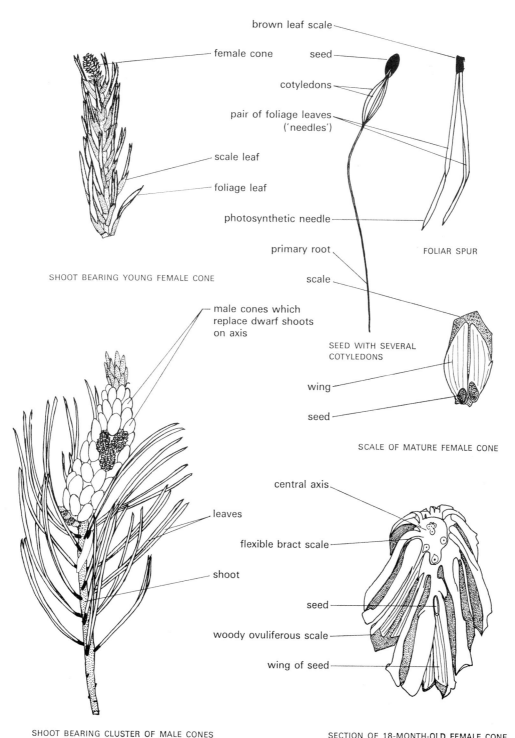

brown leaf scale

female cone

seed

cotyledons

pair of foliage leaves ('needles')

scale leaf

foliage leaf

photosynthetic needle

FOLIAR SPUR

primary root

scale

SHOOT BEARING YOUNG FEMALE CONE

male cones which replace dwarf shoots on axis

SEED WITH SEVERAL COTYLEDONS

wing

seed

SCALE OF MATURE FEMALE CONE

leaves

shoot

central axis

flexible bract scale

seed

woody ovuliferous scale

wing of seed

SHOOT BEARING CLUSTER OF MALE CONES

SECTION OF 18-MONTH-OLD FEMALE CONE

Drawing of Specimen 114

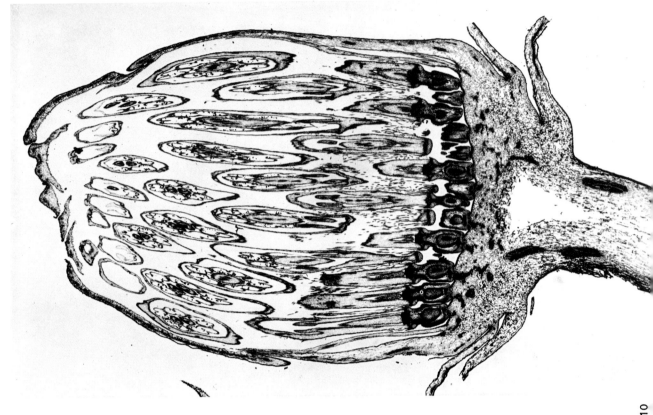

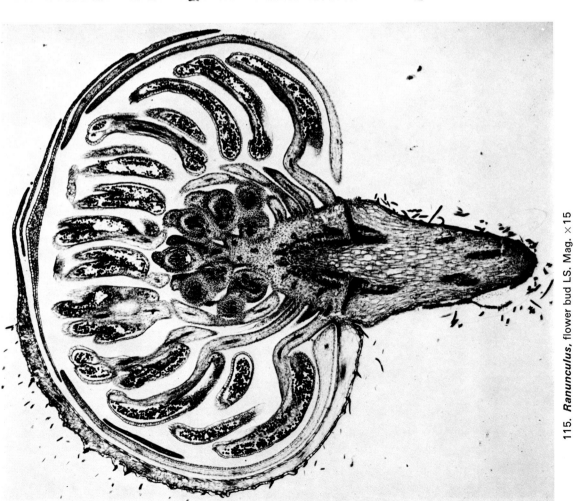

115. *Ranunculus*, flower bud LS. Mag. ×15

116 *Taraxacum*, flower bud LS. Mag. ×10

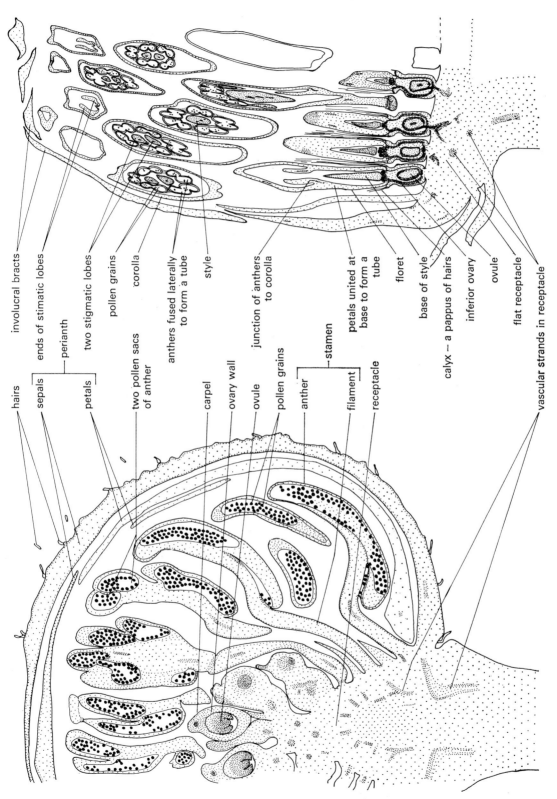

hairs

sepals ⎤
          ⎥ perianth
petals ⎦

two pollen sacs
of anther

carpel

ovary wall

ovule

pollen grains

anther ⎤
         ⎥ stamen
filament ⎦

receptacle

involucral bracts

ends of stimatic lobes

two stigmatic lobes

pollen grains

corolla

anthers fused laterally
to form a tube

style

junction of anthers
to corolla

petals united at
base to form a
tube

floret

base of style

calyx – a pappus of hairs

inferior ovary

ovule

flat receptacle

vascular strands in receptacle

Drawing of Specimen 116

Drawing of Specimen 115

87

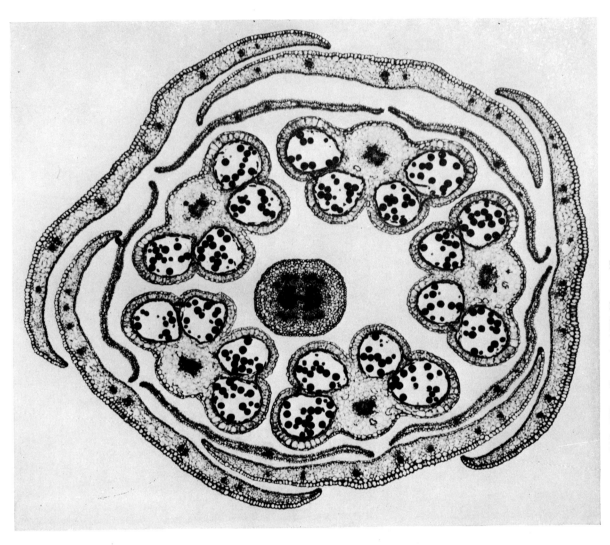

118. *Ribes,* flower bud TS. Mag. ×45

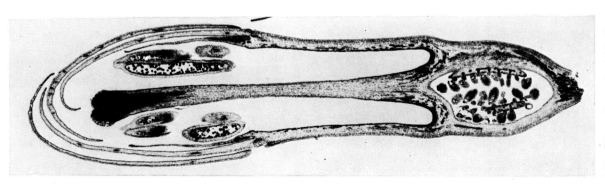

117. *Ribes,* flower bud LS. Mag. ×14

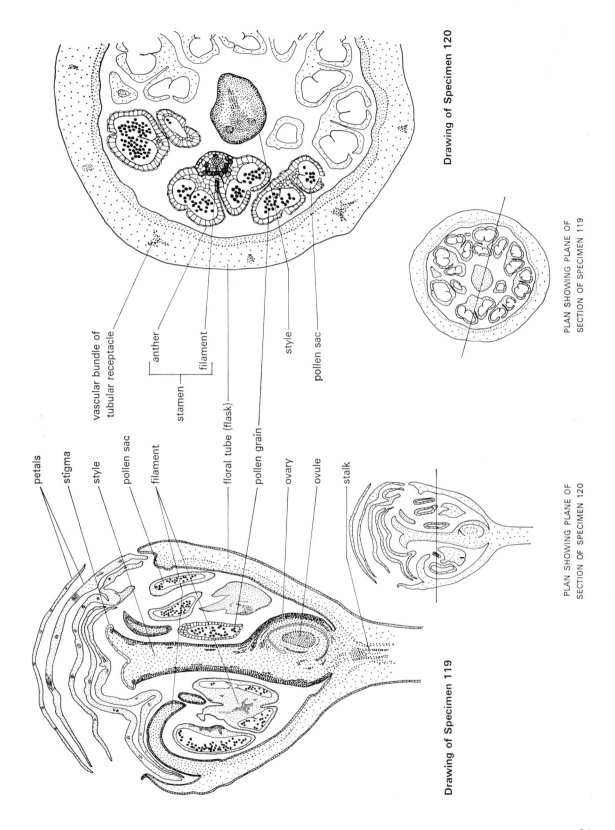

Drawing of Specimen 120

PLAN SHOWING PLANE OF
SECTION OF SPECIMEN 119

petals

stigma

style

pollen sac

filament

floral tube (flask)

pollen grain

ovary

ovule

stalk

vascular bundle of
tubular receptacle

anther

filament

stamen

style

pollen sac

Drawing of Specimen 119

PLAN SHOWING PLANE OF
SECTION OF SPECIMEN 120

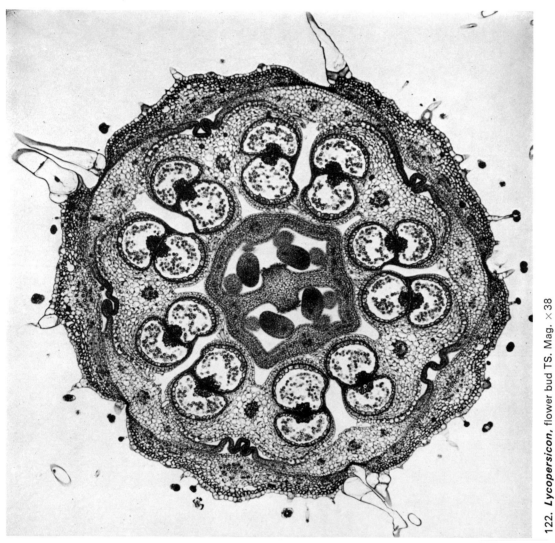

122. *Lycopersicon,* flower bud TS. Mag. ×38

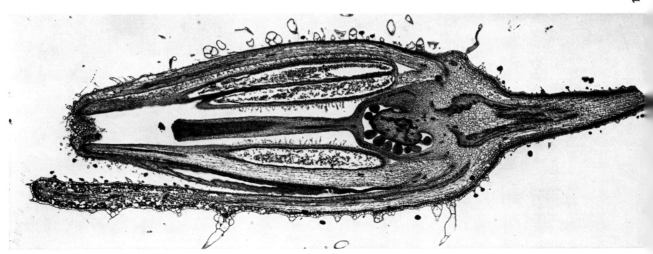

121. *Lycopersicon,* flower bud LS. Mag. ×12

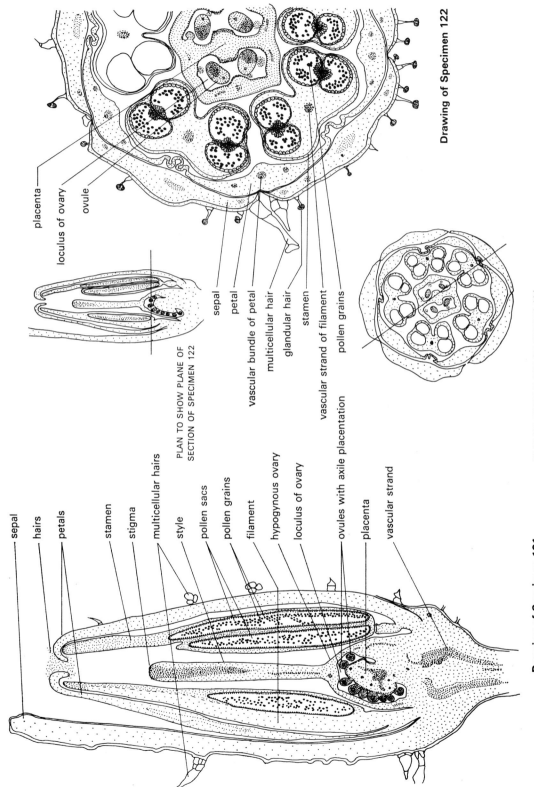

Drawing of Specimen 122

placenta

loculus of ovary

ovule

PLAN TO SHOW PLANE OF
SECTION OF SPECIMEN 122

sepal

petal

vascular bundle of petal

multicellular hair

glandular hair

stamen

vascular strand of filament

pollen grains

PLAN TO SHOW PLANE OF SECTION 121

sepal

hairs

petals

stamen

stigma

multicellular hairs

style

pollen sacs

pollen grains

filament

hypogynous ovary

loculus of ovary

ovules with axile placentation

placenta

vascular strand

Drawing of Specimen 121

93

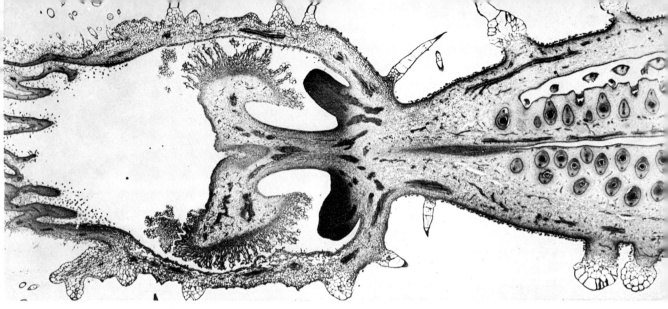

123. **_Cucumis_,** flower bud, floral nectary LS. Mag. ×8

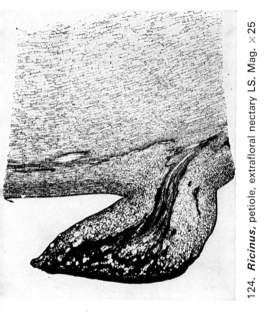

124. **_Ricinus_,** petiole, extrafloral nectary LS. Mag. ×25

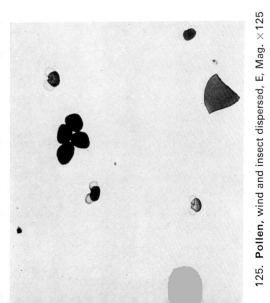

125. **Pollen,** wind and insect dispersed, E, Mag. ×125

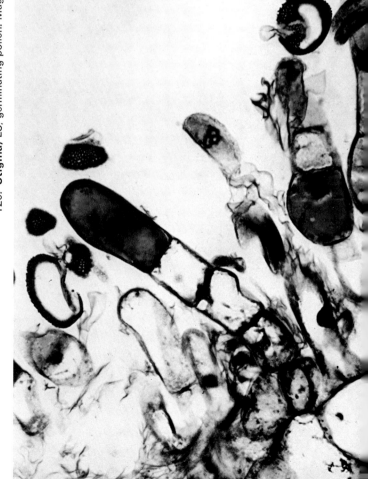

126. **Stigma,** LS, germinating pollen. Mag. ×350

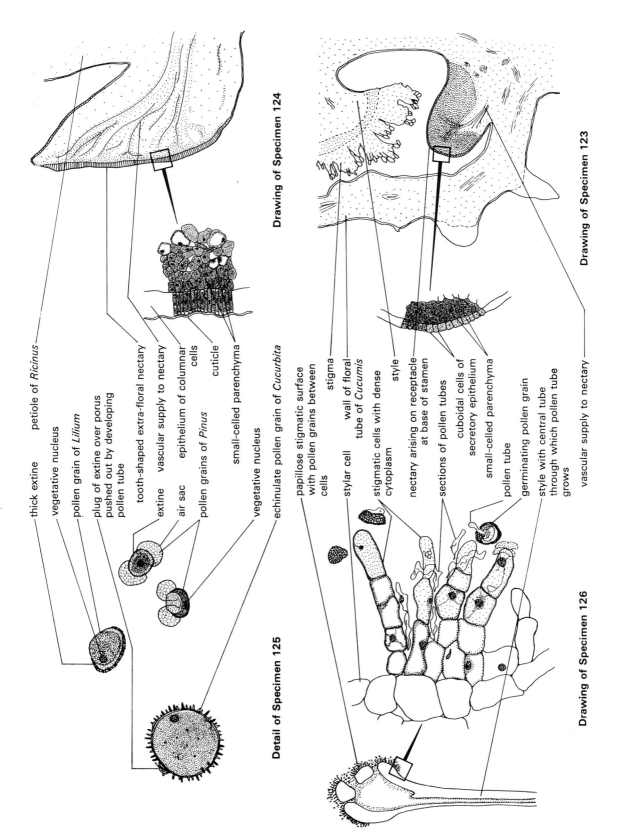

Drawing of Specimen 124

Drawing of Specimen 123

thick extine

vegetative nucleus

pollen grain of *Lilium*

plug of extine over porus pushed out by developing pollen tube

tooth-shaped extra-floral nectary

vascular supply to nectary

extine

air sac

pollen grains of *Pinus*

epithelium of columnar cells

cuticle

small-celled parenchyma

vegetative nucleus

echinulate pollen grain of *Cucurbita*

Detail of Specimen 125

papillose stigmatic surface with pollen grains between cells

stigma

stylar cell

wall of floral tube of *Cucumis*

style

stigmatic cells with dense cytoplasm

nectary arising on receptacle at base of stamen

sections of pollen tubes

cuboidal cells of secretory epithelium

small-celled parenchyma

pollen tube

germinating pollen grain

style with central tube through which pollen tube grows

vascular supply to nectary

Drawing of Specimen 126

95

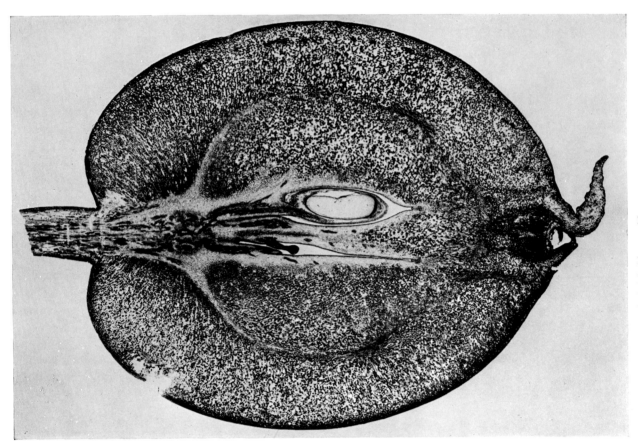

128. **Pyrus malus,** apple fruit LS. Mag. ×10

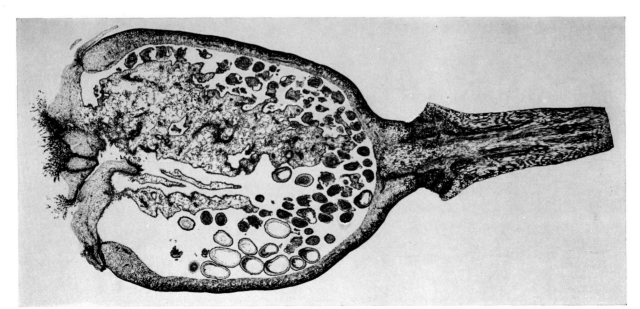

127. **Papaver,** capsule LS. Mag. ×16

cuticle
epidermis
collenchyma

unicellular hairs of stigma

stigmatic ray of crown

fruit stalk

epidermis

collenchyma

parenchymatous flesh of fruit
derived from floral tube
(hypanthium)

point at which crown upturns
to allow dehiscence of seeds

branch of sepallary bundle

carpellary bundle

placenta

funicle

placenta with seeds attached

carpellary tissue – exocarp

ovary wall lined with sclereids
– endocarp

seeds

fruit wall

lignified epidermis and
collenchyma cells

point of abscission of petals and
sepals

petallary bundle

petallary and sepallary bundle

flower stem

locule

seed

integument

locule

boundary of carpel

remains of corolla

Drawing of Specimen 128

Drawing of Specimen 127

97

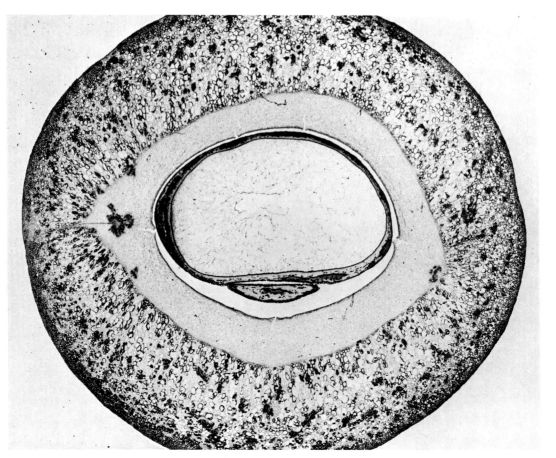

130. *Prunus*, fruit TS. Mag. ×18

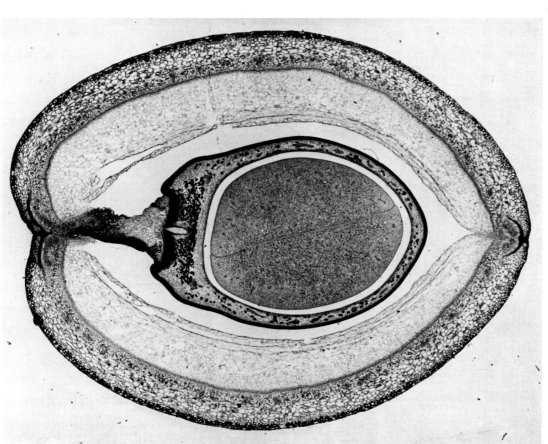

129. *Phaseolus*, pod TS. Mag. ×14

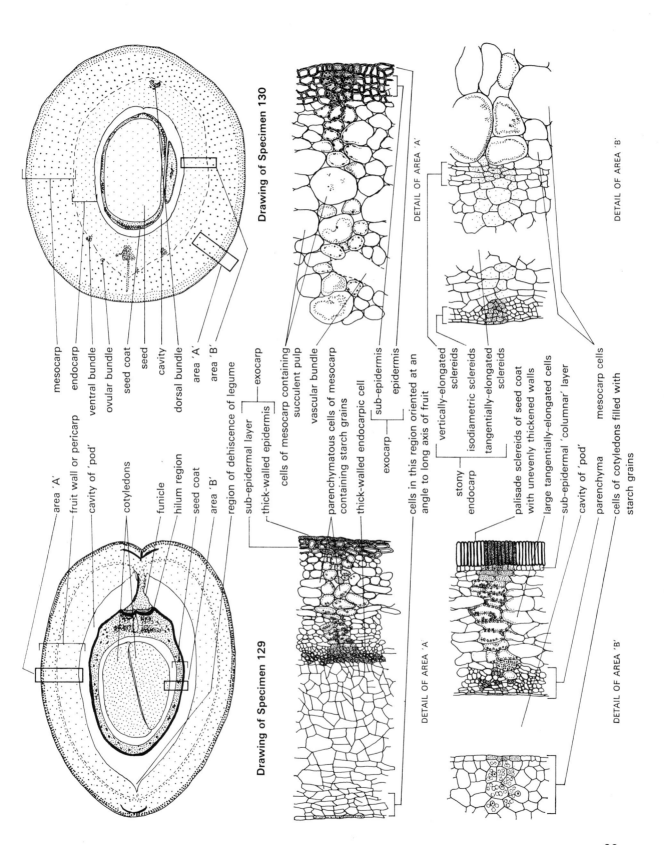

Drawing of Specimen 130

area 'A'

mesocarp
endocarp
ventral bundle
ovular bundle
seed coat
seed
cavity
dorsal bundle
area 'A'
area 'B'

sub-epidermal layer — exocarp
thick-walled epidermis

cells of mesocarp containing succulent pulp

vascular bundle

parenchymatous cells of mesocarp containing starch grains

thick-walled endocarpic cell

sub-epidermis
epidermis

exocarp

cells in this region oriented at an angle to long axis of fruit

DETAIL OF AREA 'A'

vertically-elongated sclereids
isodiametric sclereids
tangentially-elongated sclereids

DETAIL OF AREA 'B'

area 'A'

fruit wall or pericarp
cavity of 'pod'

cotyledons

funicle
hilum region
seed coat
area 'B'
region of dehiscence of legume

Drawing of Specimen 129

stony endocarp

palisade sclereids of seed coat with unevenly thickened walls

large tangentially-elongated cells

sub-epidermal 'columnar' layer

cavity of 'pod'

parenchyma   mesocarp cells

cells of cotyledons filled with starch grains

DETAIL OF AREA 'A'

DETAIL OF AREA 'B'

99

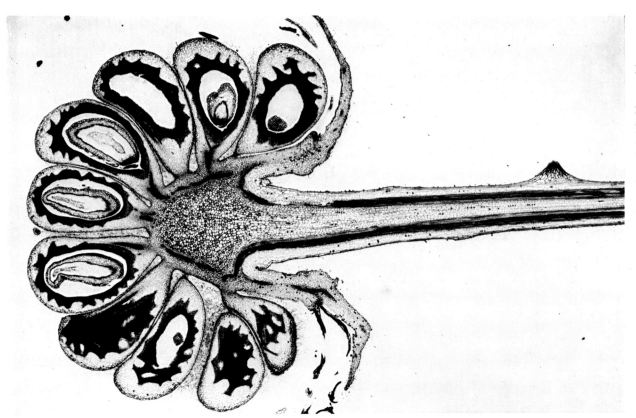

132. *Rubus*, fruit LS. Mag. ×14

131. *Xanthium*, fruit LS. Mag. ×12

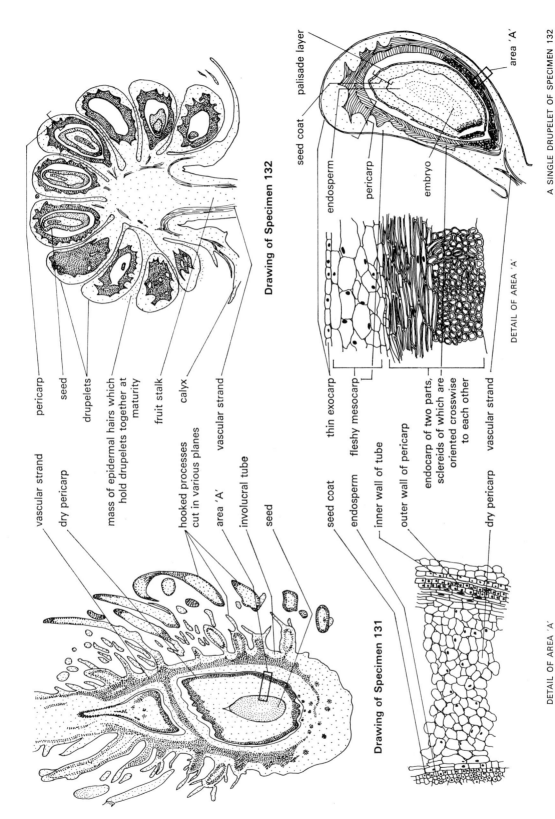

vascular strand

dry pericarp

pericarp

seed

drupelets

mass of epidermal hairs which
hold drupelets together at
maturity

fruit stalk

calyx

vascular strand

Drawing of Specimen 132

hooked processes
cut in various planes

area 'A'

involucral tube

seed

Drawing of Specimen 131

seed coat

endosperm

inner wall of tube

outer wall of pericarp

endocarp of two parts,
sclereids of which are
oriented crosswise
to each other

vascular strand

dry pericarp

seed coat

thin exocarp

endosperm

fleshy mesocarp

pericarp

embryo

seed coat

palisade layer

endosperm

pericarp

A SINGLE DRUPELET OF SPECIMEN 132

DETAIL OF AREA 'A'

DETAIL OF AREA 'A'

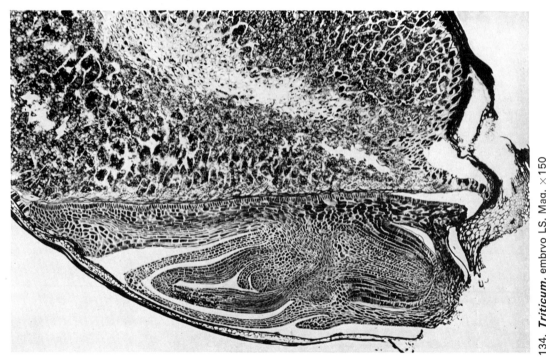

134. *Triticum,* embryo LS. Mag. ×150

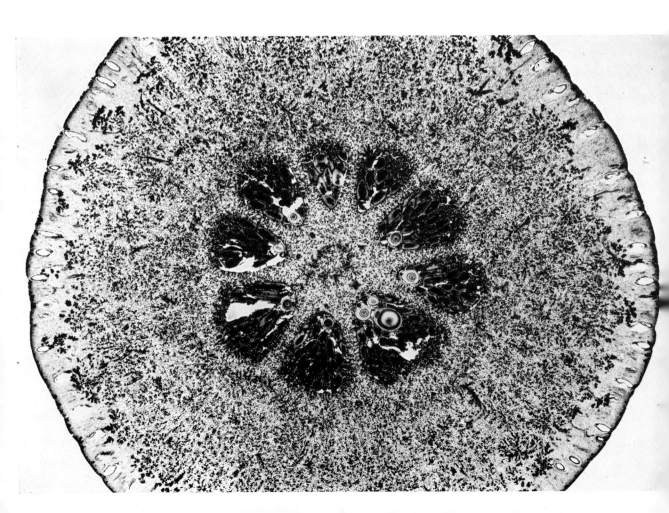

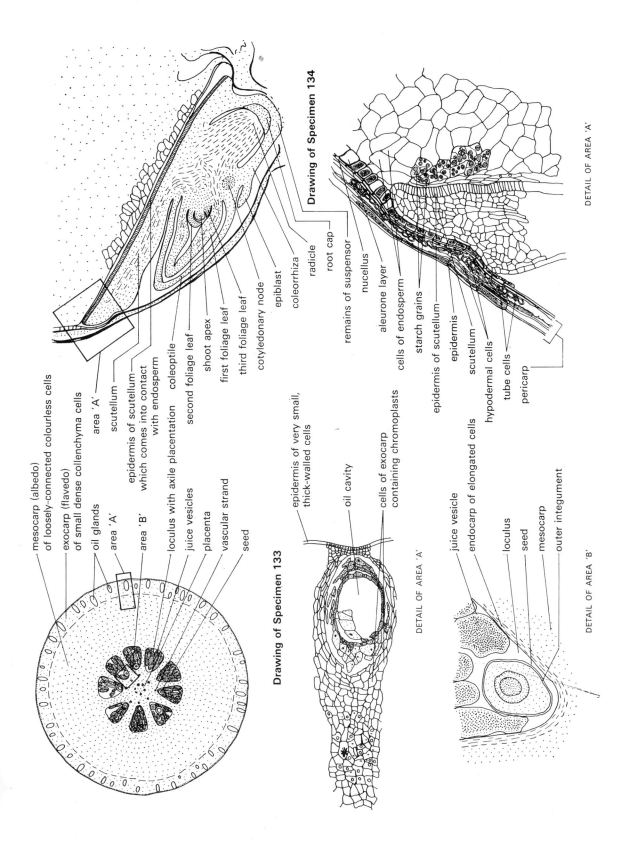

mesocarp (albedo)
of loosely-connected colourless cells

exocarp (flavedo)
of small dense collenchyma cells

oil glands

area 'A'

area 'B'

loculus with axile placentation

juice vesicles

placenta

vascular strand

seed

Drawing of Specimen 133

area 'A'

scutellum

epidermis of scutellum
which comes into contact
with endosperm

coleoptile

second foliage leaf

shoot apex

first foliage leaf

third foliage leaf

cotyledonary node

epiblast

coleorrhiza

radicle

root cap

Drawing of Specimen 134

remains of suspensor

nucellus

aleurone layer

cells of endosperm

starch grains

epidermis of scutellum

epidermis

scutellum

hypodermal cells

tube cells

pericarp

DETAIL OF AREA 'A'

epidermis of very small,
thick-walled cells

oil cavity

cells of exocarp
containing chromoplasts

DETAIL OF AREA 'A'

juice vesicle

endocarp of elongated cells

loculus

seed

mesocarp

outer integument

DETAIL OF AREA 'B'

103

135. **Angiosperms,** dicots, gross specimens. Mag. ×2

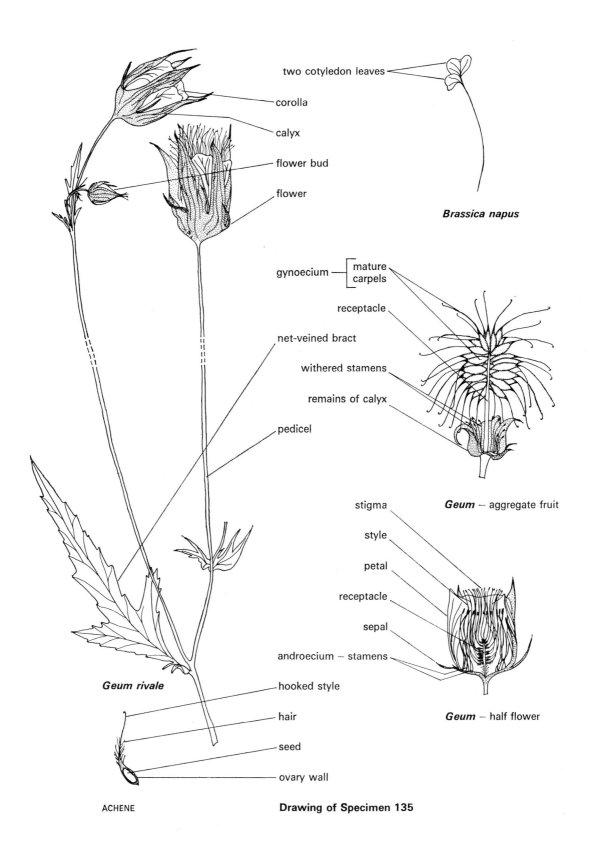

two cotyledon leaves

corolla

calyx

flower bud

flower

Brassica napus

gynoecium — mature carpels

receptacle

net-veined bract

withered stamens

remains of calyx

pedicel

Geum — aggregate fruit

stigma

style

petal

receptacle

sepal

androecium — stamens

Geum rivale

hooked style

hair

seed

ovary wall

Geum — half flower

ACHENE

Drawing of Specimen 135

136. Angiosperms, monocots, gross specimens. Mag. ×2

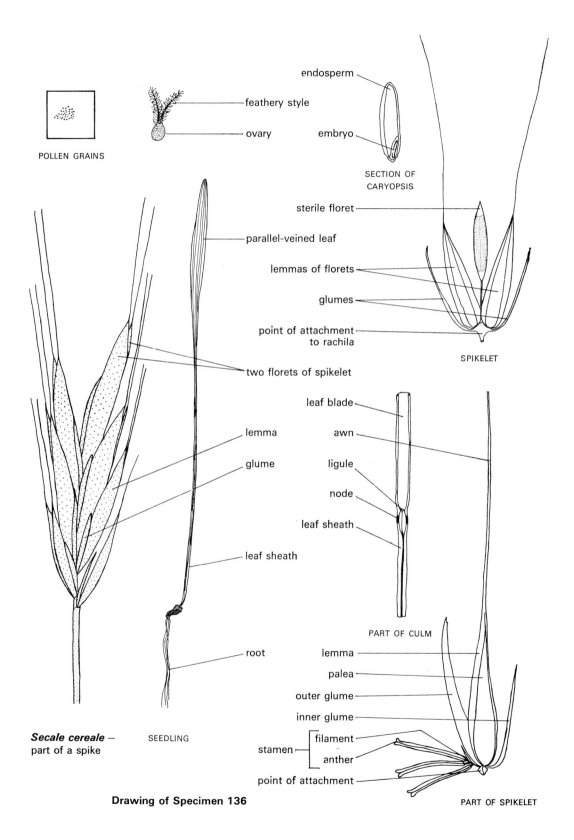

POLLEN GRAINS

endosperm

feathery style

ovary

embryo

SECTION OF
CARYOPSIS

sterile floret

parallel-veined leaf

lemmas of florets

glumes

point of attachment
to rachila

SPIKELET

two florets of spikelet

lemma

glume

leaf sheath

root

leaf blade

awn

ligule

node

leaf sheath

PART OF CULM

lemma

palea

outer glume

inner glume

stamen — filament
        anther

point of attachment

PART OF SPIKELET

Secale cereale –
part of a spike

SEEDLING

Drawing of Specimen 136

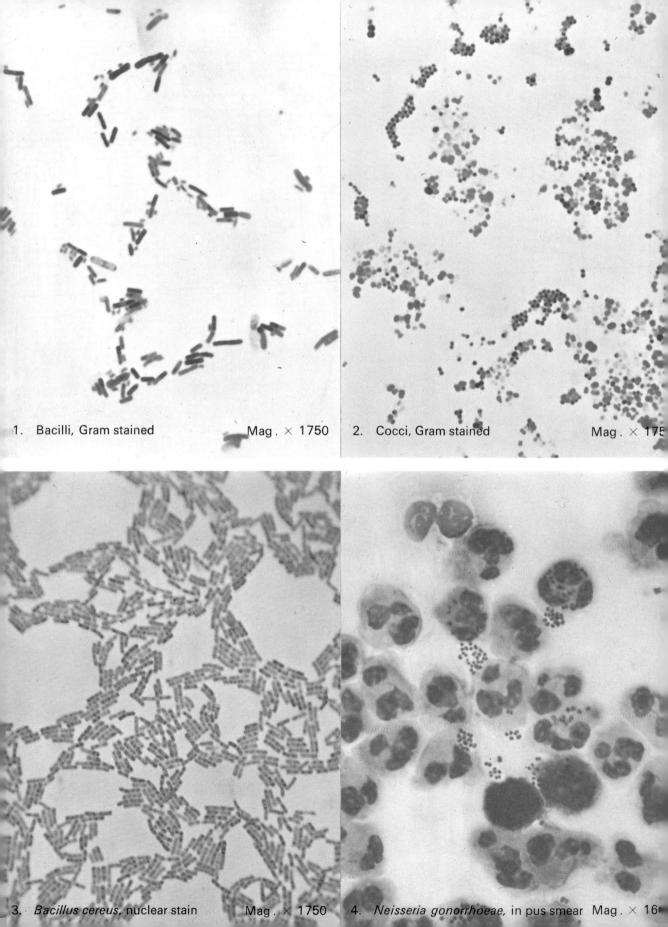

1. Bacilli, Gram stained   Mag. × 1750

2. Cocci, Gram stained   Mag. × 1750

3. *Bacillus cereus,* nuclear stain   Mag. × 1750

4. *Neisseria gonorrhoeae,* in pus smear Mag. × 16